CONAN®

THRONE OF AQUILONIA

Writer ROY THOMAS

Pencils by MIKE HAWTHORNE (chapters 1, 2, 5, 6)
DAN PANOSIAN (chapters 3, 4)

Inks by JOHN LUCAS (chapters 1, 2, 5, 6)
DAN PANOSIAN (chapters 3, 4)

Colors by DAN JACKSON

Letters by
RICHARD STARKINGS
and COMICRAFT'S JIMMY BETANCOURT

Cover and Chapter-Break Artist
ALEKSI BRICLOT

Creator of Conan
ROBERT E. HOWARD

DARK HORSE BOOKS®

Publisher MIKE RICHARDSON Designer ALLYSON HALLER Digital Production JASON HVAM and MATT DRYER Assistant Editor BRENDAN WRIGHT Editor DAVE MARSHALL

Special thanks to FREDRIK MALMBERG, JOAKIM ZETTERBERG, and LESLIE BUHLER at CONAN PROPERTIES.

This volume collects issues #7 through #12 of the Dark Horse Comics monthly *Conan: Road of Kings* series.

Published by Dark Horse Books
A division of Dark Horse Comics, Inc.
10956 SE Main Street
Milwaukie, OR 97222

DarkHorse.com

To find a comics shop in your area, call the Comic Shop Locator Service toll-free at 1-888-266-4226

First softcover edition: January 2013
ISBN 978-1-59582-905-4

10 9 8 7 6 5 4 3 2 1

Printed in China

CHAPTER ONE

"You were right, Cimmerian.
Each of us gets what he wants."

AS MITRA IS MY WITNESS, PRINCE ARPELLO...
WITH THIS DAMNED DROUGHT, EVERY STARVELING LOWLIFE ON THE CONTINENT BELIEVES HE CAN CROSS INTO AQUILONIA WITH IMPUNITY!
HALT AND IDENTIFY YOURSELF, OUTLANDER!
Of Princes and Plotters

I'M BUT A WANDERER WHO CROSSED THE RIVER TYBOR FROM OPHIR, SOME LEAGUES BACK.
THE ROAD OF KINGS DOES LIE THIS WAY, DOES IT NOT?
I'LL ASK ANY QUESTIONS THAT NEED ASKING, DOG.
GET OUT OF THE WAY SO MY LORD CAN PASS!
SINCE, AS ANY FOOL CAN SEE, I'M ALREADY HALFWAY ACROSS, ALL YOU NEED DO IS STAND ASIDE TO LET ME PASS...
...AND I'LL BE OUT OF YOUR WAY, AND ON MINE.
BEHIND THAT BARBAROUS ACCENT, DON'T YOU UNDERSTAND AQUILONIAN?
I SAID MOVE YOUR CARCASS-- NOW!
TO GET OUT OF YOUR PATH...I'D HAVE TO JUMP OFF THE BRIDGE.
THEN JUMP!
I'D RATHER NOT.
YOU DON'T SEEM TO HAVE MADE MUCH OF AN IMPRESSION ON THIS VAGABOND, LT. GARALDI.
I'LL MAKE AN IMPRESSION ON HIS GUTS, MY PRINCE--

--WITH THE POINT OF MY SWORD!
HAH!
NOW THE FROG MAKES READY TO HOP, HEY?
RRATCCCH
HNNH!?
KRAKK

SPLUSSSH
YOU SPAWN OF A NORTHRON SLUT--!
I TRUST, PRINCE--ARPELLO, I BELIEVE YOUR LACKEY NAMED YOU--THAT I MAY COMPLETE MY CROSSING OF THE BRIDGE?
COME AHEAD, WAYFARER.
JUST KEEP YOUR SWORD SHEATHED.
WHO ARE YOU, AND WHERE ARE YOU BOUND?
I AM CONAN, A CIMMERIAN.
I'M HEADED FOR MESSANTIA, CAPITAL OF ARGOS.
I'VE HEARD THAT A BORDER WAR BETWEEN ARGOS AND ZINGARA MAY BE IN THE OFFING...
...AND I'M THINKING OF HIRING MY SWORD OUT FOR A TIME.
ALAS, PELLIA, WHERE YOU NOW ARE, DOES NOT ALLOW TRAVELERS TO RANDOMLY TRAVERSE ITS LANDS.
YET I'M TOLD PELLIA IS MERELY A PROVINCE OF AQUILONIA... ONE AMONG SEVERAL...
...AND NOT A KINGDOM UNTO ITSELF.
PELLIA, LIKE POITAIN IN THE KINGDOM'S SOUTH, MOSTLY GOES ITS OWN WAY...
...AS LONG AS IT PAYS TAXES AND TRIBUTE TO THE KING WHO SITS IN TARANTIA.

NOW, WE'VE WASTED QUITE ENOUGH TIME HERE...

I LIKE THE WAY YOU HANDLE YOURSELF, CIMMERIAN.

AND I'D WAGER YOU CAN WIELD THAT SWORD JUST AS WELL.

THERE ARE MEN IN HELL WHO WOULD AGREE WITH YOU, PRINCE.

THEN FORGET THIS "MESSANTIA" BULLROAR-- AND JOIN MY ELITE GUARD.
I'LL PAY YOU BETTER THAN THE ARMY OF ARGOS OR ZINGARA.
MY PRINCE! THIS BRUTE IS A BARBARIAN--
--A COMMONER!
AND WHAT WERE YOU BUT A COUNTRY BUMPKIN WHEN I TOOK YOU AWAY FROM YOUR PIGPENS?
WELL, CIMMERIAN? WHAT DO YOU SAY?
YOUR OFFER GENEROUS, PR ARPELLO... BU LIKE TO KEEP FREEDOM.
AND, IF THE SPIRIT MOVED ME TO DO SO...
...AN ARMY IS AN EASIER THING TO DESERT THAN AN ELITE GUARD.
WELL, PERHA WE'LL THINK O WAY TO CHAN YOUR MIND
NOT AN HOUR LATER...
THERE'S THE HOVEL WE SEEK, MY PRINCE.

PEASANT--KNOW THAT YOU ARE IN THE PRESENCE OF ***PRINCE ARPELLO.***

WHAT...MAY I DO FOR YOU, MY PRINCE?

WHAT YOU ***SHOULD*** HAVE DONE LONG SINCE--

E ME THE LEVY F ***CROPS*** YOU VE ME, FOR THE WORKING OF THIS LAND.

MILORD--THE ***DROUGHT***--MY YIELD HAS BEEN SO POOR--

I'VE ONLY ENOUGH FOOD TO FEED MY OWN FAMILY, AND THAT NOT WELL.

THEN YOU SHOULD SLIT THE THROAT OF ONE OR TWO OF THOSE BRATS.

THEN YOU'D HAVE CROPS ENOUGH LEFT OVER TO PAY WHAT YOU OWE.

THAT I WILL NOT DO, MILORD.

I'M A ***FREE AQUILONIAN,*** NOT A SLAVE... AND THE ***KING'S OWN LAW*** SAYS--

"THE KING'S OWN LAW"?

I'LL SHOW YOU WHOSE WORD IS LAW IN PELLIA!
WHAT--!?
DO YOU MEAN TO DEFY ME, CIMMERIAN?
I TOLD YOU HE WAS NOT TO BE TRUSTED, MY PRINCE! LET ME--
IF YOU KILL HIM, PRINCE ARPELLO, HIS WIDOW AND SPROUTS WON'T BE ABLE TO WORK THE LAND AND PAY THE LEVY, EITHER.
TRUE ENOUGH--BUT I AM OWED WHAT I AM OWED.
SO WHAT DO YOU SUGGEST?
FELLOW--IF YOU'RE SPARED, CAN YOU TIGHTEN YOUR ROPE BELT AND PAY YOUR PRINCE IN BITS AND PIECES?
SAY, BY BRINGING A LITTLE TO HIS PALACE, EACH FORTNIGHT?
Y-YES... I THINK...
I WOULD MANAGE THAT... SOMEHOW.

YOU SEE? EACH OF YOU GETS WHAT HE WANTS.
I'LL ACCEPT THE BARGAIN YOU'VE PROPOSED...AND SPARE HIS LOUSE-INFESTED HEAD...

...IF YOU WILL JOIN MY ELITE GUARD.

AGREED.

YOU WERE RIGHT, CIMMERIAN.
EACH OF US GETS WHAT HE WANTS.
AND NOW...TO TARANTIA!

MY PRINCE...YOU KNOW THAT OUTLAND DOG WILL JUST TRY TO DESERT THE FIRST CHANCE HE GETS!
THEN IT WILL BE YOUR PLEASURE, GARALDI...

...TO KILL HIM IF HE TRIES!

TWO DAYS' RIDE, AND THE PROUD RAMPARTS AND PROUDER SPIRES OF **TARANTIA,** QUEEN CITY OF AQUILONIA, CAME INTO MAJESTIC VIEW.
THIS WAS A CAPITAL IN WHOSE FAR CORNERS **SHADIZAR THE WICKED** COULD HAVE CROUCHED SULKING, AND HARDLY BEEN NOTICED...
...AND IT SUDDENLY BECAME EASY TO CREDIT TALES OF THE ENVY WHICH THE COURT IN NEMEDIA'S **BELVERUS** FELT FOR THOSE WHO RULED IN HER SISTER KINGDOM.
CROM...
YOU CAN CLOSE YOUR MOUTH NOW, BARBARIAN.
UNLESS YOU ***WANT*** IT TO BECOME A SNARE FOR FLIES.
CONAN WAS SO STAR-STRUCK BY THE SIGHT THAT HE DID NOT HEAR GARALDI'S WORDS...

THROUGH THE GLEAMING GATES... DOWN BROAD, TEEMING AVENUES... ONTO A QUIETER SIDE STREET...

...THE CIMMERIAN BEHELD THE MARVELOUS SIGHTS OF THE GREAT CITY...

...AND THEY BEHELD HIM.

I SWEAR THEY'RE GROWING THEM *BIGGER* IN THE PROVINCES EVERY YEAR.

HE'D BE A WHOLE LOT SMALLER WHEN *WE* GOT THROUGH WITH HIM!

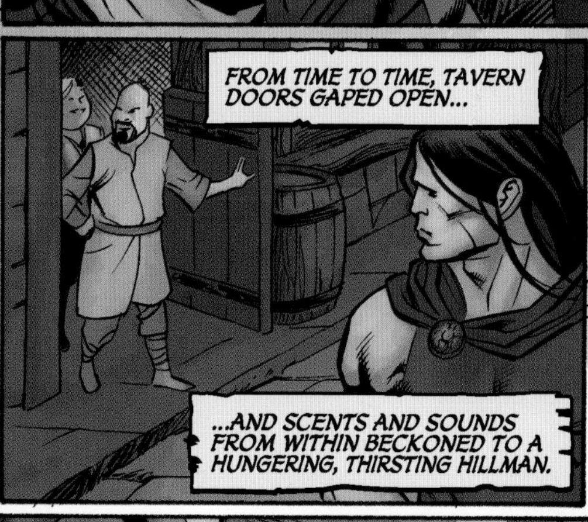

FROM TIME TO TIME, TAVERN DOORS GAPED OPEN...
...AND SCENTS AND SOUNDS FROM WITHIN BECKONED TO A HUNGERING, THIRSTING HILLMAN.

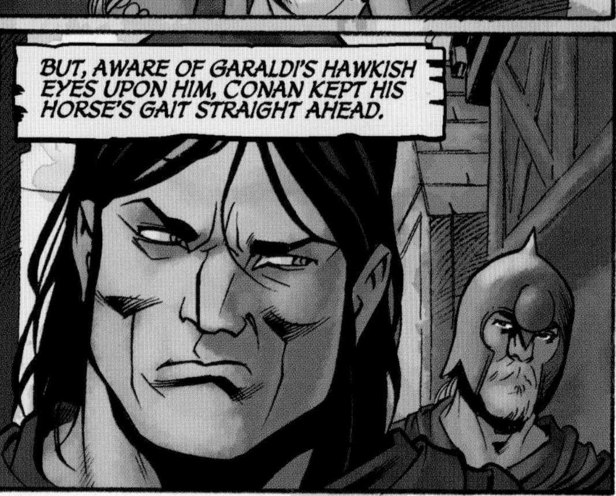

BUT, AWARE OF GARALDI'S HAWKISH EYES UPON HIM, CONAN KEPT HIS HORSE'S GAIT STRAIGHT AHEAD.

THEN, AFTER A SEEMING ETERNITY...
YOUR PRIVATE DINING CHAMBER STANDS READY AS ALWAYS, PRINCE ARPELLO.
THAT'S WHAT I PAY YOU FOR, CUR.

MY LORD...MAY I BE EXCUSED FOR A PERSONAL ERRAND?
ALL RIGHT, GARALDI...BUT DON'T BE TOO LONG.
YOU KNOW WE'VE THINGS TO DO TONIGHT THAT WILL NOT WAIT.

THE FOOD AND DRINK IN THE EIGHT-POINTED STAR WERE WELL WORTHY OF WHATEVER RETAINER ARPELLO PAID TO HAVE THE PLACE EVER AT HIS MOMENT'S BECK AND CALL.
NOR HAD CONAN ANY DOUBT THAT OTHER ITEMS, AS WELL, WERE ON THE BILL OF FARE.
PERHAPS, HE MUSED, HE WOULD NOT DESERT FOR A DAY OR TWO, AFTER ALL...
SO, GARALDI-- YOU FINALLY DECIDED TO REJOIN US?
AS SOON AS I COULD, MY PRINCE. AND WITH AN APPETITE--
--THAT WILL HAVE TO BE ASSUAGED AT A LATER HOUR.
IT IS TIME WE WERE ABOUT THE NIGHT'S BUSINESS.
YES... MY PRINCE.
AS ARPELLO'S MINIONS AROSE ALMOST IN UNISON, CONAN WAS SUDDENLY AWARE THAT HE WAS THE ONLY MAN PRESENT WHO DID NOT KNOW PRECISELY WHAT "BUSINESS" THE PELLIAN PRINCE WAS TALKING ABOUT.

BUT HE KNEW IT WOULD BE IMPRUDENT TO INQUIRE...
SO HE MERELY RODE WITH THE OTHERS THROUGH STREETS THAT DREW THEM EVER FURTHER FROM THE CONCENTRATION OF THE TALLER TOWERS...
...TILL THE RISING MOON SHONE DOWN UPON A DARKENED EDIFICE CLEARLY BUILT TO HOUSE SUPPLIES AND WARES, NOT MEN AND WOMEN...
THIS WAY, MY PRINCE.
PASSING INSIDE, CONAN FELT HE HAD BEEN IN SUCH A PLACE BEFORE:
THE HOUSE OF ANTIQUITIES IN NUMALIA HAD HOUSED MORE ICONS AND STATUARIES THAN THIS STRUCTURE, PERHAPS...
...BUT NOT THAT MANY MORE.
THAT REPOSITORY HAD BEEN HOME, AS WELL, TO DEATH IN THE FORM OF A MAN-HEADED SERPENT.
HE DARED HOPE NONE OF THESE RELICS WOULD COME EERILY TO LIFE AND LEAP SAVAGELY FOR HIS THROAT.

THEY'LL BE IN THIS INNER CHAMBER, MY PRINCE...
...WHERE NO LIGHT CAN ESCAPE TO BETRAY US.
GREETINGS, PRINCE ARPELLO.
I HATE TO BE THE ONE TO POINT OUT THAT YOU ARE A WEE BIT LATE...
PRINCES EXIST TO BE WAITED UPON, PRIEST J'HONN... IN ONE WAY OR ANOTHER.
SO YOU ARE ALL HERE.
GOOD.
I HAD HALF SUSPECTED THAT PERHAPS ONE OR MORE OF YOU MIGHT HAVE LOST STOMACH FOR OUR HOLY ENTERPRISE.
HOW "HOLY" IT IS WILL BE SEEN, ARPELLO...WHEN WE LEARN IF GREAT MITRA WILL BATHE US IN THE DIVINE LIGHT OF SUCCESS...
...OR HURL US SHRIEKING INTO THE LOWER DARKNESS, FROM WHICH EVEN HIS FAITHFUL PRIEST'S VOICE WILL NEVER REACH HIM.
YOU RELY TOO MUCH UPON THE GODS, J'HONN.
COUNT TROCERO SENT ME HERE WITH THESE MEN TO FIND OUT IF HE'S CAST HIS LOT WISELY...
...OR IF HE IS ROLLING BONES THAT HAVE BEEN WEIGHTED AGAINST HIM BY THE DEVIL.
YOU ARE YOUNG, CAPTAIN PROSPERO...BUT I SEE YOU'VE EARNED YOUR REPUTATION FOR SPEAKING PLAINLY.
HUSH, ALBIONA.
YOU BROUGHT YOUR CHILD WITH YOU, THELITIS?
WE PLAY NO GAMES HERE TONIGHT.
THERE WAS NO ONE ON MY ESTATES THAT I COULD TRUST TO LEAVE HER WITH, ARPELLO...
...NOT SINCE KING DEUCALION HAD MY NOBLE HUSBAND EXECUTED ON CHARGES AS FALSE AS A WANTON'S SMILE.

VERY ELL, WOMAN. HAT'S DONE IS DONE.
WE MUST ROCEED WITH HE MATTERS AT HAND.
TAGNAN, I MUST GO OUTSIDE AND RELIEVE MYSELF.
STAND HERE WITH YOUR BACK TO THE CLOSED DOOR TILL I RETURN AND GIVE THE PASSWORD.
AYE, LT. GARALDI.

LET US NOT MINCE WORDS.

E *SHORTER* CONCLAVE, E SAFER... SIDERING ITS URPOSE.

INDEED, PRINCE ARPELLO.

EVEN IN THE LESS METROPOLITAN HINTERLANDS OF GUNDERLAND, IT'S DANGEROUS WORK--

--TO SEEK TO *OVERTHROW A KING!*

NOT A KING, GOOD J'HONN--BUT A *TYRANT!*
DEUCALION SEEKS TO BRING YOUR *GUNDERLAND...* ARPELLO'S *PELLIA...* AND COUNT TROCERO'S *POITAIN...* UNDER HIS RUTHLESS ROYAL HEEL...
...LEAVING THEM NO AUTONOMY!

"AUTONOMY"? DON'T HONEY COAT WORDS, PROSPERO.
WHAT TROCERO WANTS IS FOR HIS POITAIN TO REGAIN THE INDEPENDENCE IT ONCE HAD.
WHATEVER MITRA WILLS.
BUT THE ROUGHER-HEWN NOBILITY OF MY NATIVE PROVINCE ALSO GRUMBLE TO SEE THE PRODUCE OF OUR FORESTS AND MINES FLOW SOUTH TO TARANTIA.
AND WHAT OF YOU, MILADY?
YOU KNOW FULL WELL WHAT I WANT, ARPELLO.
THE HEAD OF THE MURDERER DEUCALION-- THRUST ON A BLOODY PIKE, ABOVE THE GATES OF THE CITY!
AND MANY WILL FLO TO YOUR BANNE BECAUSE YOUR LA AND VALIANT LOR WAS RESPECTED BY ALL...
...AND BECAU OF YOUR OW BLUE BLOOD, COURSE.
WE ARE ALL OF O ACCORD, THE
...KING DEUCALION MUST DIE!
SO THIS, CONAN PONDERED, WAS THE CLUSTER OF NIGHT PLOTTERS IN WHOSE COMPANY HE FOUND HIMSELF.
SLY ARPELLO SOUGHT OTHERS TO DO HIS FIGHTING FOR HIM--DESPITE THE FACT THAT THE CIMMERIAN HAD HEARD ONE OF HIS LACKEYS WHISPER THAT HE WAS ALREADY CALLED "THE BUTCHER OF PELLIA."
J'HONN, LIKE OTHER PRIESTS HE'D KNOW MIXED PERHAPS SINCERE DEVOUTNESS W A PRACTICAL STREAK THAT USED RELIGIO AS A MASK FOR POLITICAL MOTIVES.
PROSPERO SEEMED EVERY INC THE NOBLE SOLDIER, READY TO MARCH INTO HELL IF AN OVERLO HE RESPECTED SHOULD DEMAND
AND THELITIS WOULD STOP AT LITTLE--IF THAT--TO GAIN THE VENGEANCE SHE SAW AS JUSTICE.
CLEARLY, THE LITTLE GIRL--WHATEVER HER NAME WAS--WAS THE ONLY INNOCENT ONE IN THE CHAMBER.

THUNKT
URGGGGG
I-- I'M--
THROW DOWN YOUR WEAPONS, TRAITORS--
--AND PLEAD FOR THE KING'S MERCY!

DEUCALION'S ELITE GUARD!
HOW DID THEY KNOW--?
THAT ONE'S ARPELLO--HE'S THE RINGLEADER!
GARALDI--YO BETRAYED ME!?
YOU MEN--TO ME!
AND ABRUPTLY, ALL WAS CHAOS.
J'HONN WIELDED AN IRON BALL MACE--FOR PRIESTS WERE NOT SUPPOSED TO SHED BLOOD.
BUT IT DID, ALL THE SAME.
PROSPERO, NOT SURPRISING WAS THE FIRST TO DRAW SCARLET WITH A SWORD...
BUT CONAN WAS ONLY A HEARTBEAT BEHIND.
HE HAD NO HOUND IN THIS FIGHT, BUT HE KNE THAT TO THE INTRUDER HE WORE ARPELLO'S BRA SO HE LIVED OR DIED WITH THE CONSPIRATO
HE PREFERRED TO LIVE.

VISIONS FLASHED FLEETING BEFORE HIS EYES...SCENES LIT BY LIGHTNING AT MIDNIGHT:
FIRST THELITIS CRADLING HER CHILD, AS IF THOSE WHITE ARMS COULD SHIELD EITHER FROM A THRUSTING SWORD...
...THEN GARALDI CUTTING DOWN A PELLIAN WITH WHOM, AN HOUR BEFORE, HE'D SHARED A RIBALD JOKE.
AND SUDDENLY, ABOVE EVERYTHING ELSE IN THIS MAD WORLD--
--CONAN WANTED TO SHEATHE HIS BLADE IN GARALDI'S GUTS!
BUT SEVERAL OF DEUCALION'S ELITE BARRED HIS WAY--
--SO THEY WOULD HAVE TO DIE **FIRST!**

PRINCE ARPELLO, MEANWHILE, HAD HIS OWN STRATEGY...
OVER HERE!
LADY THELITIS--HURRY!
I MIGHT HAVE KNOWN YOU'D HAVE A BOLTHOLE, PELLIAN.
BUNNY...
ALBIONA--
GRAB MY HAND!
LET ME GO, ARPELLO!
I NEED YO
NOT YOU
BRAT!
OUT OF HIS EYE'S CORNER, CONAN SAW THAT PROSPERO WOULD NOT MAKE FOR THE TRAPDOOR--
AARRRR
--UNTIL THE LAST OF HIS POITANIANS FELL.
WHAT OF THE REST OF YOUR MEN, ARPELLO?
THEY'RE DYING TO PROTECT ME.
THAT'S WHAT THEY WERE HERE FOR.
AS HE HEARD THE TRAPDOOR BAR SLIDE INTO PLACE BELOW--
--CONAN KNEW IT WAS TIME FOR THE LAST MAN STANDING TO FLEE--
--AND THE DOOR TO ESCAPE LAY MOMENTARIL
UNGUARDED.

THOUGH NOT PERHAPS AS EASY TO PASS THROUGH AS HE MIGHT HAVE THOUGHT.
WHEN THE SHE-DOG FLEES--
--DO NOT NEGLECT TO SLAY HER WHELP!
NO!
COME ON, GIRL--
IT'S TIME WE WERE AWAY FROM THIS SLAUGHTERHOUSE!

AS IT HAPPENED, A TRIO MORE OF DEUCALION'S FINEST LOUNGED JUST OUTSIDE.
THE CLAMOR INSIDE HAVING DIED DOWN, THEY HAD ALLOWED THEMSELVES TO RELAX THEIR GUARD.
FOR TWO OF THEM, AT LEAST, IT WOULD BE THEIR FINAL MISJUDGMENT.
THEN CONAN WAS OFF INTO THE MOON-SHOT NIGHT BEYOND--
--AND PERHAPS HE SENSED, EVEN AS HE RAN--
--THAT HE WAS CARRYING A HEAVIER BURDEN THAN EVER HE HAD LIFTED BEFORE.

CHAPTER TWO

"You turned pale, barbarian . . . I saw it, even in the dark.
Did you hear of this 'Acheron' before?"

DAMN.
BEL'S HELLS!
BY CROM--
--I THINK I'VE GOT IT!
The Horrors beneath the Stones

CAN YOU COOK A CHICKEN ON SUCH A LITTLE FIRE?
IF YOU *HAD* A CHICKEN?
KEEP IT DOWN, GIRL. SOMEONE WILL HEAR.

I'M HUNGRY...
...AND I WANT MY MOMMY...
...AND MY NAME IS *ALBIONA.*

YOU SAW YOUR MOTHER FLEE, WITH THE OTHERS... DOWN THE TRAPDOOR.
AND A *CURSE* ON ANYONE WHO'D DRAG A *CHILD* INTO THEIR CONSPIRACY!
SHE RAN AWAY...*LEFT* ME.

ARE *YOU* GOING TO LEAVE ME, TOO?

YES, I AM.

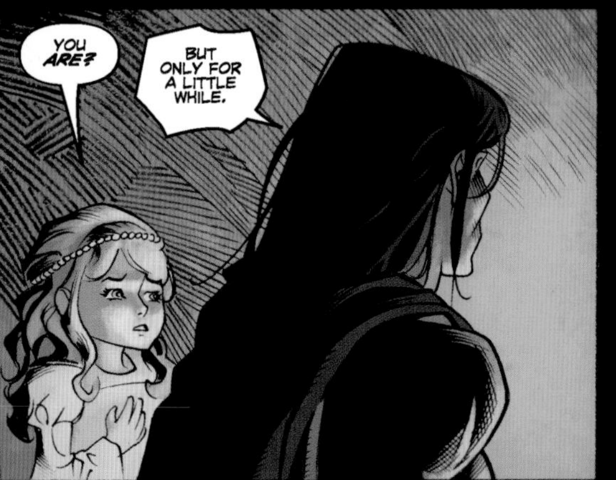
YOU *ARE?*
BUT ONLY FOR A LITTLE WHILE.

DIDN'T YOU SAY YOU WERE *HUNGRY?*

ROTHGOR! I THINK WE'VE LOST THEM!
KEEP MOVING! EVEN IF THOSE MANSERVANTS CAN'T SEE OUR TRACKS IN THE DARK--
--THEY MIGHT STILL FIND US BY FOLLOWING THEIR NOSES!
MMMM! I CAN ALMOST TASTE THESE VITTLES NOW.
EVEN THE BREAD IS STILL WARM!
TO ME, THIS PASTRY'S THE CREAM OF TONIGHT'S PICKINGS!
SERVES THAT FAT MERCHANT RIGHT, FOR HAVING MORE THAN WE DO!
AND YOU, AT THE MOMENT, HAVE MORE THAN I DO.
WH--?
WHO THE DEVIL ARE YOU?

WHAT'S IT MATTER? HE IS ONE. WE ARE TWO.
I'D LIKE THAT FOOD YOU STOLE...
...BEFORE IT COOLS OFF.
WHAT YOU'LL GET IS A PAIR OF BLADES IN YOUR GIZZARD!

WE'LL SEE.

...ALBIONA...

DID YOU SAY YOU LIKED CHICKEN?

I'VE TAKEN A BITE OUT OF *THIS* LEG...
BUT THERE'S ANOTHER ONE...
...AND PLENTY MORE FOOD, BESIDES.
...WHOEVER COOKED THIS BIRD HAS A TALENT.
AND THIS PASTRY LOOKS TO BE SWEETER THAN A CIMMERIAN MAIDEN'S FIRST KISS.
HERE, CHILD.
IF I EAT ANY MORE, MY BELT WILL SPLIT IN TWO.
THANK YOU... BARBARIAN.
WHY DID YOU CALL ME "*BARBARIAN*"?
THAT'S WHAT MY *MOMMY* WHISPERED TO ME THAT YOU WERE.
I DON'T KNOW WHAT IT *MEANS*...
BUT IT MUST NOT BE *TOO* BAD.

AND NOW THAT OUR BELLIES ARE FULL...
...IT'S TIME I WENT TO FIND YOUR MOTHER AND HER FELLOW PLOTTERS.
YOU STAY RIGHT HERE!
THK
DID YOU HEAR--
CAP'N SAID HE'D HAVE OUR BALLOCKS IF ANYTHING GETS IN OR OUT OF WHERE THOSE CONSPIRATORS ARE TRAPPED...
...SO IT'D TAKE MORE'N A SCURRYING RAT TO PRY ME FROM THIS POST.

ARE YOU SOLDIERS--
--OR DID YOUR MOMMIES JUST DRESS YOU FUNNY?
WHAT'S THIS?
SOME HARLOT'S BRAT, MOST LIKE.
MY MOMMY'S INSIDE THERE--
SO YOU JUST GET OUT OF MY WAY!
HEY-- DIDN'T THEY SAY THERE WAS A LITTLE GIRL WITH THE TRAITORS?
COME BACK HERE, SPROUT!
GET HER!
OHHHHH...
Y-YOU KEEP AWAY--!
KLONKK

I THOUGHT I TOLD YOU TO STAY PUT.
I WANTED TO *HELP* YOU.

WELL...MAYBE YOU *DID*... JUST A LITTLE.
IF NOT FOR YOU, I'D HA
HAD TO *RUSH* THESE
FOOLS, AND MAKE A LO
MORE NOISE.
SO, LONG AS YOU'RE HERE...

...WE'D BEST GO IN *TOGETHER*.
TO FIND MOMMY?

AND HER FRIENDS.

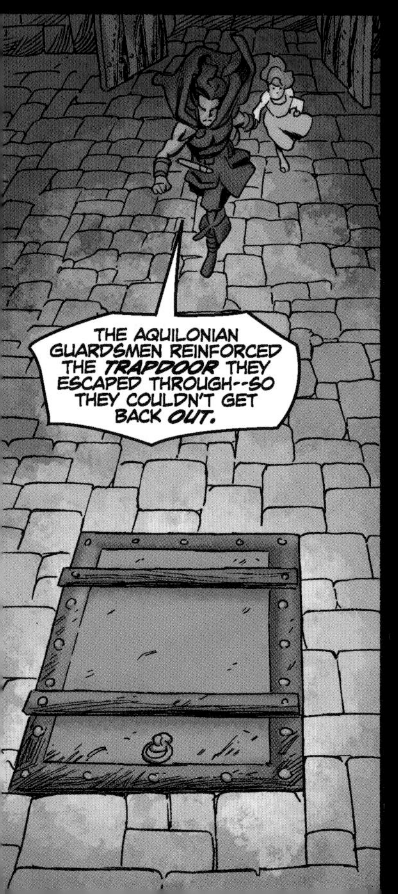
THE AQUILONIAN GUARDSMEN REINFORCED THE *TRAPDOOR* THEY ESCAPED THROUGH--SO THEY COULDN'T GET BACK *OUT*.

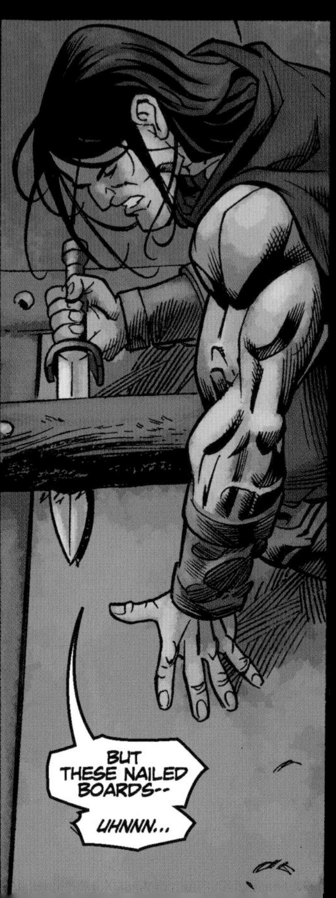
BUT THESE NAILED BOARDS--
UHNNN...

--WON'T STOP ME--
KRRIK

--FROM GOING *IN!*
IT'S SO... *DAAARRRK.*
I DIDN'T *FORCE* YOU TO COME ALONG.
BUT WE'D BETTER KEEP TO *WHISPERING* AGAIN...
WE DON'T KNOW *WHO* OR *WHAT* MIGHT BE DOWN HERE...
THIS ISN'T JUST SOME *BOLTHOLE* YOUR MOTHER AND HER COHORTS DUG OUT WITH THEIR FINGERNAILS.
I THINK...
I THINK THIS MUST BE THE *CATACOMBS.*

HERE ARE THE *TRACKS* OF THE CONSPIRATORS-- OR AT LEAST *SOMEONE'S.*
THESE ARE *MOMMY'S!* SEE? THEY'RE *LITTLER* THAN THE OTHERS.
GOOD EYE, ALBIONA.
BUT--YOU MENTIONED *"CATACOMBS"*-- BURIAL CHAMBERS...
MOMMY TOLD ME ABOUT THEM...
SHE SAID, LONG AGO, THE FOLKS WHO LOVED THE GOD *MITRA* CAME DOWN HERE TO *PRAY* TO HIM.
THEY WERE *HIDING...* BECAUSE THEY WERE SLAVES...
...SLAVES OF A BAD EMPIRE THAT *RULED* THIS LAND BACK THEN.
AND WHAT WAS THIS *"BAD EMPIRE"* CALLED?
IK-KIRA...
OH-KER-OHN...
SOMETHING LIKE THAT.
OH...*NOW* I REMEMBER...
ACHERON!
IT WAS CALLED *ACHERON!*
YOU TURNED *PALE,* BARBARIAN... I SAW IT, EVEN IN THE DARK.
DID YOU HEAR OF THIS *"ACHERON"* BEFORE?
ONLY FEARFUL WHISPERS THAT OLD MEN SAY THEY HEARD ECHOING DOWN THE BLACK CORRIDORS OF TIME.
KEEP MOVING.
AND CALL ME *CONAN,* NOT *"BARBARIAN"!*

YES, THIS IS THE CATACOMBS, RIGHT ENOUGH!
THOSE MITRA WORSHIPERS--THE ANCESTORS OF THE AQUILONIANS--MUST HAVE CARVED THE BURIAL SPACES RIGHT OUT OF THE ROCK--
--AND LAID THEIR DEAD THEREIN, TO AWAIT THE COMING OF THE LAST LIGHT.
ONLY-- WHERE ARE THE REMAINS?
THERE ARE NO SKELETONS...
NO TATTERED REMNANTS OF LONG-ROTTED CLOTHING...
NOTHING BUT BAUBLES CARVED IN THE SHAPE OF THE BRIGHTENING SUN...
NOT EVEN PILES OF DUST INTO WHICH SKULLS AND SHINS AND RIB CAGES MIGHT HAVE CRUMBLED OVER THE CENTURIES.
CONAN...I'M S-SCARED...
YOU'D BE A SILLY YOUNG FOOL IF YOU WEREN'T.

STAY CLOSE! WE MUST KEEP MOVING.
WE KNOW WHAT AWAITS US ABOVE IN TARANTIA.
AT LEAST, AHEAD MAY LIE A WAY THAT EMERGES OUTSIDE ITS WALLS.
HOLD!
I THOUGHT I SAW SOMETHING MOVE IN THAT BURIAL SHELF.
YES! THERE'S SOME KIND OF GAPING CRACK IN THE REAR OF IT.
AND...THERE'S SOMETHING...
KKKKKKKKKKKKKKKKKKKKK
YYAAAAAA
EEEEEEE

KKKKKKKKKKKK
BURN, YOU VERMIN--
--OR IS STEEL MORE TO YOUR LIKING?
DIE, DEVIL--
--AND LET YOUR DEMON SOUL SLITHER BACK DOWN--
--TO WHATEVER BLACK HELLS SPAWNED YOU!
MACHA, MORRIGAN, AND NEMAIN!
IT WAS--LIKE A MANY-LEGGER--ONLY BIG AS A PYTHON!
STILL, ONCE I SAW IT WAS NOT A PHANTOM, BUT A LIVING CREATURE--AN ANIMAL--I KNEW IT COULD BE KILLED!
C-CONAN...

KKKKKKKKKKK
KKKKK
KKKK
CAN YOU KILL ALL THOSE, TOO, PLEASE?
FSSHHFSSHH
FFSSHHH
RRRIK
RRRIKRRRIK
KKKKKKKKKK

CROM TAKE ME--
SO THIS IS WHAT ATE FLESH AND BONE AND MARROW OFF THE AQUILONIANS!
KKKKKKKKKKKKKKKKKK
THEY'VE CLOSED IN BEHIND US, AND ON BOTH SIDES--BUT THE WAY AHEAD LIES MOSTLY CLEAR--FOR THE MOMENT--
AND THEY RECOIL--A LITTLE--FROM THE LIGHT.
TAKE THE TORCH--SO YOU CAN SHINE OUR PATH AHEAD, AND SHOW ME WHAT TO STRIKE.
WHEN I GIVE THE WORD, RUN ALONG BESIDE ME WITH THE TORCH-- AND DON'T LOOK BACK.
AND KEEP ON RUNNING--EVEN IF I AM NO LONGER BESIDE YOU!
I'LL... TRY.
NOW!
RUN!

WHATEVE
HAPPENS
DON'T
STOP!
CONAAAAAAN
RRRIKRRRRIK
RRRIK
KEEP GOING--

I DON'T SEE ANY OF THESE DEVILS BEYOND THAT DOORWAY!
WE CAN HOLD THEM OFF FROM THERE! FOLLOW ME!
KKKKKKKKKKKKKKKKKKKKKKK
OHHH--
DON'T WORRY, GIRL.
I SAID I WOULDN'T LEAVE YOU!
GET UP HERE--
--OUT OF REACH OF THE ONES THAT CLAMBER ALONG THE FLOOR--
--WHILE I DO MY WORK!

KK
KK
K
K
KK
K
CONAN--!
SSLASSSSH
YOUR LEGS-- THEY'RE--
CLOSE YOUR EYES, GIRL--
--AND WHATEVER YOU DO--WHATEVER YOU HEAR OR FEEL--
DON'T OPEN THEM!
RRRIK RRRIKRRRIK

TKK TKK TKK TKK TKK
I-I WON'T! BUT--
THERE'S SOMETHING--
TKK TKK TKK
FWOOOSH
TKKKKK
ALBIONA--
WHAT ARE YOU DOING HERE, AMONG THESE HELLISH CREATURES?
I WAGERED YOU'D BE HALFWAY BACK TO CIMMERIA BY NOW, CONAN!
MOMMY! IS IT REALLY YOU?
IF I HAD THE SENSE THE GODS GAVE A GOBLIN, PROSPERO--

SKWISSHH
--I WOULD BE!
THE SARCOPHAGI ARE FALLING BACK--BEFORE SO MANY TORCHES.
I'LL ADMIT--WHEN I SAW YOU COVERED IN THOSE BUG-THINGS, I THOUGHT YOU BEYOND SAVING!
I TOLD YOU--HE'S MY MAN, AND TOUGH AS THEY COME!
I'M NO ONE'S "MAN," ARPELLO--LEAST OF ALL YOURS!
I SAW HOW YOU LET "YOUR MEN" DIE, WHILE YOU SCRAMBLED FOR SAFETY.
WATCH YOUR TONGUE, SAVAGE, OR I'LL--
OR YOU'LL WHAT?
CEASE YOUR SQUABBLING, YOU TWO!
AYE. I SHOULD THANK YOU ALL--EVEN YOU, ARPELLO--
--FOR SAVING WHAT'S LEFT OF MY SKIN.
HOW COULD YOU BRING MY LITTLE GIRL INTO THIS PLACE?
LITTLE CHOICE I HAD--AFTER YOU'D DRAGGED HER TO YOUR CONSPIRATORS' MEETING.
IF YOU HAD LITTLE CHOICE, BARBARIAN--
--I HAD NONE AT ALL.

SARCOPHAGI-- "FLESH DEVOURERS."

BUT OUR TORCHES WOULD ONLY HAVE HELD THEM AT BAY--NOT MADE THEM TAKE FLIGHT AS THEY DID.

THERE ARE SITUATIONS IN WHICH THE SARCOPHAGI ARE NOT PREDATORS.

WHAT ARE THEY, THEN?

--THEM!
HHNNNN...
CROM...

CHAPTER THREE

"Ah! How sweet to smash a skull and see only green filth come oozing out, for in these vermin no single drop remains of the red blood I am forbidden to shed!"

When
EATH
akes
Wing...
BEFORE US, CIMMERIAN, STANDS THE REASON THE CATACOMBS' SHELVES ARE BARREN.
THEN-- THE CORPSES THAT ONCE LAY THERE--WERE **NOT** DEVOURED BY BUGS LIKE THOSE AT OUR FEET?
J'HONN SAYS THEY ROSE FROM THEIR GRAVE-SPACES--AND WALKED AWAY!

PROSPERO! J'HONN! I AM ROYALTY!
IT IS YOUR BOUNDEN DUTY TO KEEP THOSE STALKING DEAD FROM ME!
DON'T LOOK, MY DARLING! JUST HOLD ON TO ME--!
THE COUNTESS WAS REARED IN PAMPERED LUXURY--AND ARPELLO IS USED TO HAVING OTHER MEN DIE FOR HIM--
--BUT WHY DO YOU, WHO FOUGHT SOLDIERS AND WORMS LIKE A TIGER, BLANCH AT THE SIGHT OF WALKING CARCASSES?
I'LL FIGHT MAN OR BEAST--BUT WIZARDRY TURNS MY BONES TO WATER.
IN THE ABSTRACT, BARBARIAN, I SUPPOSE I FEAR DEATH--
BAAASSH
--BUT NOT THE DEAD!
AH! HOW SWEET TO SMASH A SKULL AND SEE ONLY GREEN FILTH COME OOZING OUT--
--FOR IN THESE VERMIN NO SINGLE DROP REMAINS OF THE RED BLOOD I AM FORBIDDEN TO SHED!

WHY SHOULD A PRIEST FEAR SORCERY, MAN?
AFTER ALL, WHAT IS RELIGION--BUT MAGIC, PRESIDED OVER BY A PRIEST INSTEAD OF A WIZARD?
HAHAHAHAHAH
IN CASE YOU TWO HAVE FORGOTTEN, THERE'S STILL AN UNLIVING LEGION MARCHING UPON US, WITH LONG-ROTTED ARMS OUTSTRETCHED!
AND TOMORROW, NO DOUBT--IF I SURVIVE--I SHALL TREMBLE AT THE MEMORY OF THOSE I FOUGHT TONIGHT.
BUT, FOR JUST THIS SINGLE MOMENT, I BURN WITH SEETHING LIFE--
SWAASH
SLAASSSH
--AND I FEAR NOTHING THAT WALKS OR CRAWLS THE EARTH!
KRUNTCH
IF WE COME OUT THE OTHER SIDE OF THIS MELEE, CONAN, I MAY MAKE A PRIEST OUT OF YOU YET!
SZZSH
BY MITRA, I WAS RIGHT THE FIRST TIME!
I'M DESTINED TO DIE HERE FLANKED BY A COUPLE OF MADMEN!

ARPELLO! GET YOUR BLUE-BLOODED TAIL OVER HERE AND HELP FIGHT THESE DEVILS!
I MEAN TO KEEP MY PRINCELY BLOOD RIGHT WHERE IT IS--OVER HERE, AND INSIDE MY BODY!
WHAT IF MORE OF THEM ATTACK US FROM THE REAR?

I CAME THAT WAY, MINUTES AGO--AND ENCOUNTERED NOTHING BUT THE BUGS!

CURSE ME FOR A HYPERBOREAN--I MIGHT AS WELL HAVE TOLD HIM TO FLEE!
BARBARIAN, BEHIND YOU--!

KRAK
CROM TAKE ME--

--IS THERE NO END--

--TO THIS SURGING TIDE OF DEATH?

M-MOMMY...
SSSSSS
GET BACK, YOU DEMON IN INNOCENT'S FORM!
SSZZZZL

THELITIS--
ALBIONA--
HANG ON! I'LL TRY TO--
AARRRR
FWOOSH
HAH!
YOU DRY, DEAD DEVILS RECOIL IN FEAR FROM THAT THRUST TORCH--
--GIVING ME THE CHANCE TO RISE FROM THIS MOVING, GRASPING BURIAL MOUND--
--AND BEHOLD MY FIRE-BEARING BENEFACTOR

ALBIONA...?
I OWE YOU A DEBT, LITTLE ONE... WHICH SHALL BE PAID.
YOU SAVED ME LOTS OF TIMES... CONAN.

MITRA! YOU CHOP OFF THESE SHAMBLERS' LEGS--

--AND STILL THEY CRAWL AT YOU ON BLOODLESS STUMPS!
RUN, WALK, OR CRAWL, PROSPERO--

--THEY HAVE US IN A CORNER!

WHILE, A FEW WINDING TUNNELS AWAY...
...KEEP CALM, ARPELLO.
YOU'LL FIND A WAY OUT OF THESE ACCURSED CATACOMBS! YOU WILL!
LET'S SEE...IT WAS THIS WAY YOU FIRST CAME WITH PROSPERO AND THE OTHERS, HEY?
NO--WE MUST HAVE COME FROM OVER THAT WAY.
EH? IS THAT DAYLIGHT COMING THROUGH YONDER CRACK?
I THOUGHT WE WERE BENEATH THE CITY.
YET IT MUST BE THE LIGHT OF THE SUN...
IT MUST!
FOR WHAT ELSE--
--COULD IT BE?

WE'RE DOOMED AND DAMNED, IT SEEMS, MY FRIENDS--
--BUT, THE GODS BE OUR WITNESS, WE'LL GO DOWN FIGHTING!
IN ANOTHER DAY AND PLACE, PROSPERO, I'D HAVE BEEN CONTENT TO BATTLE KINGS AT YOUR SIDE.
IT IS GIVEN TO FEW MEN, BARBARIAN, TO CHOOSE THE TIME AND MANNER OF THEIR DEATH--
--BUT I'LL WAGER NONE WOULD ESPOUSE THIS GRISLY END!

SO-- YOU WANT TO BE NEXT TO TRY YOUR LUCK, SKULL-PATE?
WELL, THUS FAR, I'VE SWUNG A HEADS AND ARMS AND LEGS--
--BECAUSE SURELY NO HEART BEAT WITHIN SUCH BOSOMS--
SLAASSSH
--BUT YOU I'LL SLICE FROM SKULL TO TOE--
--AND SEE HOW YOU WALK THEN!
BY CROM! HE LIES AS UNMOVING AS ANY CORPSE I'VE SEEN!
SO WHY AREN'T HIS TWO HALVES STILL COMING AT ME, ON KNEES AND ELBOWS?
THERE'S THE REASON, OUTLANDER--

--THAT SMALL, EYELESS CREATURE THAT HID WITHIN ITS HOLLOW CHEST!
IT'S SCUTTLING AWAY!
TCHOK
IT WILL SCUTTLE NO MORE--
--NO, NOR SHAMBLE OR LURCH, EITHER!
THIS, THEN, IS THE SOURCE OF MOTION IN THE HUSKS OF MEN WHO DIED LONG AGO--
SOME KIND OF UNSPEAKABLE PARASITE THAT CRAWLED INTO THE MIDST OF DRIED FLESH AND CREAKING BONES--
--AND GAVE THEM AN UNHOLY SEMBLANCE OF LIFE!

SUCH KNOWLEDGE MAKES MY SKIN CRAWL!
SO WHY ARE YOU SMILING, CONAN?
BECAUSE NOW I KNOW THESE BEINGS AREN'T GHOSTS OR DEMONS--
--BUT ONLY ANIMALS, LIKE BIRDS THAT FLY AND SNAKES THAT SLITHER--
--AND I'VE NEVER YET MET THE BEAST THAT COLD STEEL WON'T CUT!
BY MITRA, WHEN YOU PUT IT THAT WAY--!
GENTLEMEN--SHALL WE?
MOMMY--DON'T CONAN AND THE OTHERS SEE HOW MANY OF THE DEAD ONES THERE ARE AGAINST THEM?
THEY'VE WILLED THEMSELVES NOT TO SEE THEIR NUMBER, CHILD.
ONLY IN THAT WAY CAN THEY FIND THE COURAGE TO GO ON FIGHTING!

BUT--SURELY THREE MEN, HOWEVER FIERCE, CANNOT HOLD OUT FOR LONG AGAINST--
RUN! RUN FOR YOUR LIVES!
EH?

PRINCE ARPELLO-- RACING AS IF PURSUED BY THE HARBINGERS OF HELL!
MOMMY-- WHAT'S ALL THOSE LIGHTS COMING BEHIND HIM?
IT'S DEATH--!
DEATH ON THE WING!

WHAT ARE THOSE GLOWING THINGS, ARPELLO?
I-- THOUGHT I'D FOUND A WAY OUT--
BUT THEY WERE SLEEPING BEHIND THE WALL--
--AND THERE'S A MULTITUDE OF THEM!
WELL, THIS LOOKS LIKE THE END, LADS.
IT'S BUT A MATTER OF WHETHER THE DEAD-WALKERS GET US FIRST--OR THOSE FLYING FIENDS!
AND YET--THERE IS SOMETHING ABOUT THE WAY THE WINGED THINGS COME--
YYAAAA! THEY HAVE ME!
FOOL! THEY ONLY KNOCKED YOU ASIDE--
--SO THEY COULD REACH THE SHUFFLING CORPSES BEHIND YOU!
IT'S NOT US THEY'R AFTER--

THEY'RE AFTER THE PARASITES WITHIN THE DEAD-WALKERS!

SURELY THAT IS WHY THE PARASITE-BEASTS DEVELOPED THE HABIT OF "WEARING" THE HUMAN CARCASSES LAID TO REST IN THE CATACOMBS--
--TO PROTECT THEMSELVES, AS BEST THEY COULD, AGAINST THE APPETITE OF THOSE FEAR-SOME FIRE-WORMS!
MAY I SUGGEST WE GET OUT OF HERE, WHILE OUR FOES PREY ON EACH OTHER?
THIS WAY, LADIES!
WHICH GROUP DO YOU THINK WILL TRIUMPH, BARBARIAN?
MY GOLD--IF I HAD ANY--WOULD BE ON THE FIRE-WORMS--
"--BUT ALL I REALLY CARE ABOUT IS THAT THEY KEEP FIGHTING TILL WE'RE GONE!"
OVER HERE, LADS AND LASSES!
I'D BEEN LOOKING FOR THIS CORRIDOR--WHEN LITTLE ALBIONA CAME RUNNING AND BEGGED US TO GO HELP THE CIMMERIAN!
DON'T LAG BEHIND, ARPELLO, UNLESS YOU WISH TO MAKE A FINAL COURSE FOR THE VICTORS.
I...AM COMING.

THESE STAIRS LEAD UPWARD-- HOPEFULLY TO THE *TRUE* LIGHT OF DAY--
--AND NOT TO MORE *WINGED PREDATORS!*

YOU SEEM TO KNOW *MUCH* ABOUT THESE CATACOMBS, J'HONN.
I MEMORIZED THEIR PLAN FROM ANCIENT SCROLLS, WHEN I STUDIED TO BECOME A PRIEST.
WHY DO YOU THINK I SUGGESTED THE WAREHOUSE ABOVE FOR OUR MEETING-PLACE?

CONAN--I SUSPECT WE WILL PART COMPANY EN WE REACH THE SURFACE, NCE YOU'VE NO PART IN OUR CONSPIRACY AGAINST KING DEUCALION.
WE WILL. WHAT DO *I* CARE WHO PARKS HIS FAT SHANKS ON AQUILONIA'S THRONE?
PLEASE KNOW-- I COULD NOT HAVE EN PROUDER TO FIGHT SIDE *ANY* MAN THAN I IAS TO STAND WITH *YOU* THIS DAY.

AND I COULD IMAGINE NO WARRIOR I'D RATHER HAVE AT MY FLANK THAN *YOU,* PROSPERO...

...UNLESS IT BE *PRIEST J'HONN* THE GUNDERMAN, OF COURSE.
THE SAME BACK *AT* YOU, CIMMERIAN!

A SHORT TIME LATER...

HAH! GOOD TO FINALLY BE ***ABOVEGROUND*** AGAIN.

I'LL BE HAPPY TO LEAVE THAT SUBTERRANEAN WORLD TO THE WORMS AND CADAVERS.

THIS OLD RUIN--WHICH WAS ONCE A GRANARY--IS FAR ENOUGH FROM THE WAREHOUSE THAT WE'VE LITTLE TO FEAR OF RUNNING INTO DEUCALION'S MINIONS.

THEN IT'S TIME I TOOK MY LEAVE ON THE ROAD OF KINGS--
--WITH A HOPE THAT YOU ALL EVADE THE KING'S SEARCHING GUARDSMEN.

WELL, BROTHERS AND SISTERS?
IS ONE OF YOU GOING TO TELL HIM--OR MUST I?

TELL ME WHAT?

IT WOULD SEEM YOUR NEWFOUND FRIENDS ARE AT A LOSS FOR WORDS, BARBARIAN.

AMN YOU, HAT ARE U TALKING AB--
EH? WHAT'S THAT RISING UPROAR OUTSIDE?
I'LL TELL YOU--SINCE NO ONE ELSE WILL.

HEN OUR LE GAGGLE ONSPIRATORS ERED IN THE HOUSE--WHAT N SEEMS A LIFETIME AGO--
--WE ERE MEETING SEEK A WAY SSASSINATE G DEUCALION--

--IF POSSIBLE, BEFORE SOMETHING ELSE HAPPENED!
THAT'S WHAT YOUR OH-SO-VALUED COMRADES NEGLECTED TO INFORM YOU.
GO ON! TELL HIM, IF YOU'RE DETERMINED TO!

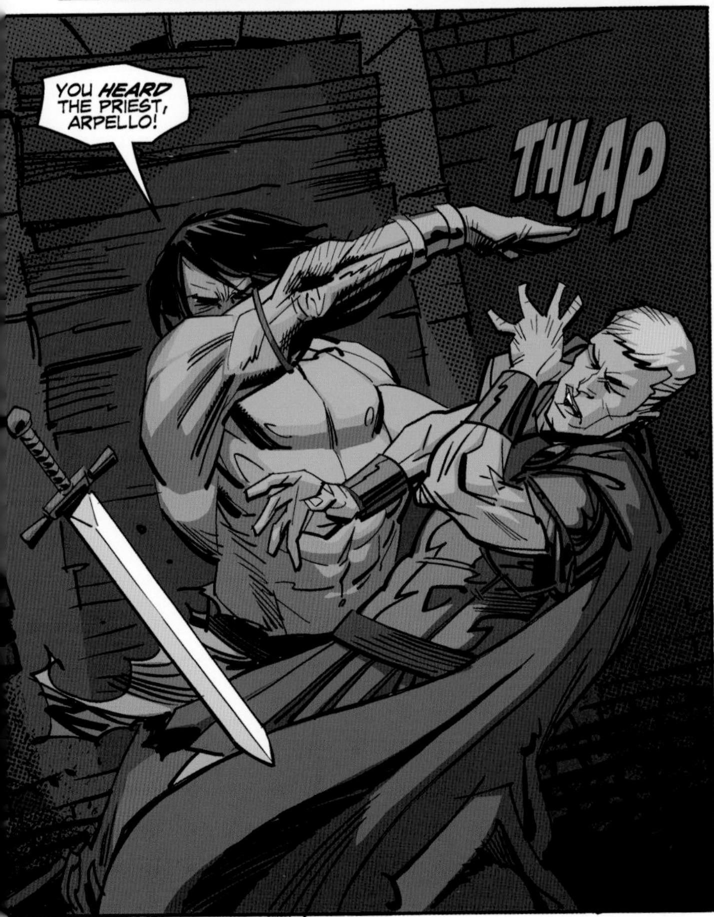
YOU HEARD THE PRIEST, ARPELLO!
THLAP

SPIT OUT THIS DIRE SECRET EVERYONE'S BEEN KEEPING FROM ME--BEFORE YOU DO IT THROUGH TOOTHLESS GUMS!
L-LOOK OUT THE WINDOW--
--AND SEE FOR YOURSELF!

FROM THE SOUND OF THINGS, THE TIMETABLE MUST HAVE BEEN MOVED UP.
WHAT TIMETABLE, POITANIAN?
FRAKKK
THE START OF THE ATTACK, CONAN!
FOR ONCE, ARPELLO SPOKE THE TRUTH:
WHAT YOU SEE LAID OUT BEFORE YOU IS TARANTIA IN TURMOIL.
WHAT'S GOING ON, PROSPERO?
TELL ME, DAMN YOU!

"CAN'T YOU GUESS, CIMMERIAN?
"MY OVERLORD, COUNT TROCERO OF POITAIN, HAS BEGUN LAYING SIEGE TO AQUILONIA'S PROUD CAPITAL.
"HE IS DETERMINED THAT, IF KING DEUCALION'S TYRANNY CANNOT BE OVERTHROWN FROM WITHIN--IT WILL BE TOPPLED FROM WITHOUT!"

THE PETTY SQUABBLES OF AQUILONIA AND ITS RESTIVE PROVINCES MEAN NOTHING TO ME.
I'LL CUT MY WAY OUT THROUGH ROYAL TROOPS AND REBELS ALIKE THAT STAND IN MY WAY...

ARE YOU GOING TO LEAVE US, CONAN?

THERE IS... NO REASON FOR HIM TO REMAIN, CHILD.

YES, ALBIONA.
I AM GOING TO LEAVE TARANTIA.

AFTER I MAKE CERTAIN OF YOUR SAFETY.
AND THUS, YOUR MOTHER'S.

TO DO THAT, YOU'D HAVE TO COME WITH US ALL--NOW--FOR THE COUNTESS IS KEY TO OUR PLAN.
WE MUST ATTEMPT TO CARRY OUT OUR PLAN TO ASSASSINATE DEUCALION--
--AND PLACE HIS NEAREST HEIR ON THE THRONE OF AQUILONIA.
AND JUST WHO IS THIS HEIR-APPARENT?
YOU KNOW HIM WELL, CIMMERIAN...

PRINCE ARPELLO OF PELLIA!

CHAPTER FOUR

"I knew that none of us—none—who walked into this palace would ever walk forth again. So I hid this dagger in my inner thigh. It was the first place he looked . . ."

PRINCE ARPELLO--
--"THE BUTCHER OF PELLIA"--
--NEXT IN LINE TO BE ***AQUILONIA'S KING?***
AND YOU WANT ME TO HELP YOU SET HIS COWARDLY BEHIND ON THE ROYAL PRIVY?
YOU MUST ALL BE ***MAD AS HYPERBOREANS!***

IT IS THE ***DUTY*** OF COMMONERS, BARBARIAN, TO SERVE THOSE OF ***REGAL BLOOD!***
SHUT UP, ARPELLO! YOU ARE NOT HELPING.
COME, COUNTESS. I'LL TRY TO GET YOU AND YOUR DAUGHTER ***OUT*** OF THIS CITY WHILE IT'S STILL STANDING.
NO! I CAME HERE TO SEE MY HUSBAND'S MURDERER SLAIN-- NOT TO FLEE BACK TO MY ESTATE!
MOMMY--I'M ***SCARED!***

Is Tarantia Burning?

DO NOT FORCE US TO FIGHT YOU, CONAN.
FOR, AS YOU SEE, THELITIS MEANS TO COME WITH US TO THE PALACE.
IF YOU'LL HELP US, MY LORD COUNT TROCERO WILL PAY YOU HANDSOMELY.

I CAN'T SPEND HIS MONEY IN HELL, PROSPERO.
BUT--I'LL STUMBLE INTO DEATH'S MAW WITH YOU FIVE--
--THOUGH, BY CROM, I'D ABANDON THE LOT OF YOU, IF NOT FOR THE GIRL!

I THINK OUR CIMMERIAN FRIEND MAY BE OF A MORE NOBLE BENT THAN HE CREDITS HIMSELF, PRIEST J'HONN.
BEST NOT LET HIM HEAR YOU SAY THAT!

BARBARIAN--I KNOW YOU'RE WONDERING WHY MY PRESENCE IS SO ESSENTIAL TO OUR CONSPIRACY.
DEUCALION LUSTS AFTER ME. THAT'S THE REASON HE HAD MY LORD KILLED.

HE WILL ADMIT ME TO HIS QUARTERS, EVEN AMID THIS SIEGE--
--AND YOU MEN WILL BE WITH ME, DISGUISED AS MY RETAINERS.
BUT WHY DRAG ALBIONA INTO THE SNAKEPIT?

I HAD TO BRING HER.
AFTER ALL, IF I PLANNED MISCHIEF AGAINST THE KING--WOULD I DARE BRING MY OWN POOR DEFENSELESS CHILD ALONG?

AND MEANWHILE, AT THE RAMPARTS OF TARANTIA, THE VIOLENT SIEGE CONTINUED REDLY...

...WITH SPEARS AND ARROWS RAINING BOTH **SKYWARD** AND **EARTHWARD**-- AS IF THE TORRENTS OF THE **HEAVENS** WERE BEING MET AND EQUALED BY CASCADES FROM THE **NETHER REGIONS.**

HALT! WHO WALKS THERE?

NO MAN--OR WOMAN--OR CHILD-- MAY ENTER THE ROYAL APARTMENTS UNLESS SENT FOR BY HIS MAJESTY!

I RECOGNIZE YOU NOW, MILADY. I MEANT NO DISRESPECT.
BUT YOU MUST KNOW THE CITY IS **BESIEGED** BY THAT DEMON, TROCERO OF POITAIN.
THE KING HAS OTHER THINGS TO DO THAN--THOSE MIGHT **WISH** TO DO.

AT PRESENT, HE IS BUSY WEIGHING HOW TO MARSHAL HIS FORCES...
HAH! THAT FOOL DEUCALION COULDN'T COMMAND AN ARMY OF **TOY SOLDIERS** COMPETENTLY!
THE KING WILL BE **WROTH** WITH YOU IF YOU REFUSE OUR ENTRANCE!
STAND ASIDE! I SHALL--
DETAIN HER!
GOOD! NOW, YOU WILL ESCORT THE COUNTESS--
--TO MY PRIVATE **CHAMBERS,** SERGEANT!

AH, THELITIS, THELITIS--I **KNEW** ONE DAY YOU WOULD STOP MOURNING THAT MILKSOP OF A HUSBAND AND COME TO ME!
AND, EVEN IN THE MIDST OF A **WAR** THAT HAS BEEN FORCED UPON ME BY UNGRATEFUL SUBJECTS--
--I AM PREPARED TO WELCOME YOU WITH **ARMS SPREAD WIDE!**

YOU KNOW, BETTER THAN ANY MAN, THE WORKINGS OF A WOMAN'S HEART, MY LIEGE.
TRUE.
YET I FEARED THAT PERHAPS--GIVEN THE CRIMSON NATURE OF THE COUNT'S DEMISE--YOU MIGHT HARBOR SUSPICIONS HE WAS A VICTIM OF MY ROYAL WILL.
EVEN WERE THAT SO, SIRE...I WOULD BE FLATTERED YOU SHOULD DESIRE ME SO GREATLY THAT NO MAN, NOT EVEN MY HUSBAND, COULD BE ALLOWED TO STAND BETWEEN US.
WE ARE NEAR ENOUGH TO STRIKE...
NO, CONAN! THERE ARE TOO MANY GUARDS.
WE MUST BIDE OUR TIME.
IT CHEERS ME YOU HAVE COME, MILADY, JUST AFTER TROCERO HAS SENT WORD I MUST ABDICATE--
--OR ELSE HIS POITANIANS WILL BATTER--OR STARVE--TARANTIA INTO SUBMISSION.
SURELY YOU WILL NOT CONSIDER SURRENDERING?
OF COURSE NOT.
THEN PERHAPS WE SHOULD RETIRE TO YOUR BED-CHAMBERS...TO CELEBRATE YOUR COMING VICTORY?
YES... OH, YES! BUT FIRST, ONE TRIFLING DETAIL...
CAPTAIN! FEED THE RETAINERS--AND THE CHILD--TO MY ROYAL DRAGON.
DRAGON? BUT SURELY, MY KING...
DO IT!

NOW?
NOW!
THERE IS TREASON HERE, LADS! TAKE THEM!
ALIVE, I COMMAND YOU!
MY PET LIKES FRESH, RED MEAT!
THEN, BY CROM--
--LET'S SERVE UP MORE THAN OUTLAND FLESH ON THAT PALACE PLATE!
UNHAND ME, MONGRELS! I AM A PRIEST OF MITRA!

KLANNG
HOLD ON, J'HONN! I SHALL--
URGGK
SO THIS, CONAN SAW, WAS HOW THE GRAND CONSPIRACY ENDED:
PROSPERO AND J'HONN DOWN--
--MORE GUARDS FLOODING IN BY THE MOMENT--
--AND ARPELLO--
SPARE ME! I AM UNARMED-- AND OF THE ROYAL LINE!
ONLY TWO THINGS, NOW, REMAINED WORTH CONTINUING THE UNEVEN STRUGGLE--

ONE WAS CAUGHT UP IN THE ARMS OF DEUCALION'S CAPTAIN-- TENDERED UP BY HER OWN MOTHER--
--WITH A WALL OF AQUILONIAN STEEL BETWEEN HER AND THE CIMMERIAN.
THE OTHER WAS HIS OWN LIFE
BETWEEN THE THOUGHT AND THE ACTION FELL NO MORE THAN A HEARTBEAT...
GET HIM!
HE'S TRAPPED, CAPTAIN! THERE'S NO WAY OUT FROM UP THERE!
WHAT IN THE GODS' NAME IS HE--

THE FOOL! HE'S LEAPING TO HIS--
--DEATH!
HIII-YAAAAAAAAAA

AAAAAAAAAA
KRASSHK
C-CROM...
I'VE NOT TAKEN SO BAD A FALL...
...SINCE I TOPPLED OFF...MOUNT MORRIGAN.

EVEN... BROKE MY SWORD...
GLANCING BACK TOWARD THE HIGH WINDOW, CONAN PONDERED HIS FRIENDS' FATE THERE...A CERTAIN DOOM...
...AND THE MELEE ABOUT HIM IN THE CITY, SCARLET AND CHAOTIC AND MEANINGLESS TO HIM.
AND SO HE STRODE RESOLUTELY BACK TOWARD THE LOOMING PALACE.
SPLANNGG
WHO'S THERE?
YOUR GUIDE TO THE DEVIL'S DOORSTEP.

YOU MEANT TO BETRAY ME!
THEY FORCED ME--AT SWORD-POINT--OR THEY'D HAVE KILLED MY CHILD.
PLEASE-- LET ME SHOW WHAT I CAN DO TO MAKE IT UP TO YOU.
I SHOULD NOT--
BUT I HAVE LONG HAD A WEAKNESS FOR THOSE LIPS, TELL THEY TRUTH OR LIES.
FROM THIS MOMENT, MY LORD, I SWEAR--
--THEY SHALL SPEAK NO MORE LIES TO YOU.
THIS WAY, ALL!
TROCERO'S BATTERING-RAM IS NIGH TO KNOCKING DOWN THE CITY'S GATES--
--AND THE KING CAN HANDLE THAT STRUMPET!
DEUCALION!

HE'S DEAD.

YOU *KILLED* HIM?
BUT HIS MEN HAVE YOUR *CHILD*--AND WE NEEDED HIM AS A *HOSTAGE!*
I KNEW THAT NONE OF US-- *NONE*--WHO WALKED INTO THIS PALACE WOULD EVER WALK FORTH AGAIN.
SO I HID THIS DAGGER ON MY INNER THIGH.
IT WAS THE FIRST PLACE HE LOOKED...

--AND THE *LASSSST*

THUS DID THE KING AND THE COUNTESS LIE TOGETHER VOLUPTUOUSLY IN DEATH...
...AS THEY NEVER QUITE DID IN LIFE.

AND CONAN REALIZED FULLY, AT LAST, JUST HOW STRONG WAS THELITIS'S HATRED OF HER HUSBAND'S SLAYER.
BUT NOW HE HAD OTHER LIVES TO SAVE, IF POSSIBLE...
...YET, ABOVE ALL, ONE.
PROSPERO'S NASTY FLESH WOUND MIGHT YET PROVE FORTUITOUS.

IN AN INSTANT, THE CIMMERIAN'S GRIM GAZE TOOK IN THE STARK TABLEAU THAT LAY BEYOND THOSE WIDE-SWINGING DOORS...
...INCLUDING THE MASSIVE REPTILIAN IN THE YAWNING PIT...
...A CREATURE DOUBTLESS DRAGGED UP TO TARANTIA FROM THE JUNGLES AND SWAMPS RUMORED TO SPRAWL SOUTH OF STYGIA AND INLAND FROM THE BLACK COAST.
HSSSSSSS

BUT HIS STEEL-BLUE EYES WERE RIVETED ON A SMALL, BLOND, WRIGGLING FORM...
CAPTAIN! LET GO OF THE GIRL--AND LIVE!
CONAN--HE'S HURTING ME!
I HAVE MY ORDERS, BARBARIAN--
SHE'S A TIDBIT FOR THE KING'S DRAGON!
EEEEEEE
ALBIONA!
AARR
I'M COMING, GIRL!
YOU SHOULD HAVE KEPT YOUR EYES ON YOUR PRISONER!
PERHAPS THE DRAGON WOULD PREFER A MAN-SIZE MEAL!
PLEASE--I'VE MADE NO MOVE TO ESCAPE...
YYYIIIII

HIISSSS
DON'T MOVE, CHILD!
O, LIZARD! I'M OVER HERE!
NO--HERE!
AND NOW--OVER HERE!
CONAN--DON'T LEAVE ME!
RRARRRR
THAT'S IT--REAR UP--
A BIT MORE, DAMN YOU--
--AND GIVE ME AN OPEN PATH--

RRAARRRRRRRRRRR
HNNNF! NOT QUITE AS TENDER AS I'D HAVE LIKED--
--BUT STILL FULL OF ENTRAILS THAT SPELL OUT YOUR DIRE FUTURE!
--TO YOUR TENDER UNDERBELLY!
IS--IS IT DYING?
PROBABLY--
--BUT I DON'T THINK WE SHOULD HANG AROUND TO FIND OUT, DO YOU?
N-NO!

NOW TO SEE WHAT KIND OF GREETING WE GET TOPSIDE!
WHAT? WILL IT TAKE PARADES TO SATISFY YOU?
JUST A HELPING HAND, PRIEST.
WHERE'S PROSPERO?
HE...HAD AN ERRAND TO RUN, AFTER WE FINISHED OFF THESE GUARDS.
F HE MEANS TO TRY TO SASSINATE AQUILONIA'S KING--THE COUNTESS BEAT HIM TO IT.
DEUCALION-- DEAD?
PRAISE BE TO MITRA!
COME! WE GO TO MEET PROSPERO.
GIRL, YOU HIDE HERE, TILL WE RETURN FOR YOU.
IS MY MOMMY HIDING, TOO?
I'LL YOU AS STRAIGHT AS I WOULD TELL A LITTLE CIMMERIAN GIRL.
SHE DIED... TO PROTECT YOU.
AH... THERE'S PROSPERO NOW.
IS IT TRUE, MAN OF POITAIN?
IS THE TYRANT DEAD-- AND IS THE CROWN MINE?

YES...
...AND NO.
BY THE GODS! THAT MAN BESIDE YOU--IS THAT NUMEDIDES?
IT IS, ARPELLO. NUMEDIDES--DEUCALION'S YOUNGER COUSIN.
GREETINGS, SIRE, FROM A HUMBLE MAN OF MITRA.
I HAD NO IDEA NUMEDIDES WAS A GUEST IN THE PALACE.
BUT YOU AND J'HONN KNEW, DIDN'T YOU, PROSPERO?
OH, YES, CONAN.
LESS A GUEST--THAN A PRISONER UNDER PALACE ARREST.
YET THAT PUT YOU IN JUST THE RIGHT PLACE--FOR YOUR CORONATION.
TREACHERY
YOU TWO USED ME--NEVER INTENDING TO SET ME ON THE THRONE!
I'LL HAVE BOTH YOUR HIDES FOR--
SO NOW YOU FINALLY DRAW YOUR SWORD--WHEN IT IS FAR TOO LATE TO DO ANYONE ANY GOOD--EVEN YOURSELF.
OOOPH!
THOK
YOU SHOULD HAVE KNOWN WE NEED A SUCCESSOR OF FULL ROYAL BLOOD--AND WELL-LIKED BY THE POPULACE.
THEY WOULD NEVER ACCEPT A RUTHLESS PRINCE FROM PELLIA, A MERE PROVINCE--ANY MORE THAN THEY WOULD ACCEPT A POITANIAN.

YOU'VE NOTHING TO FEAR FROM ME, ARPELLO--SO LONG AS I HAVE YOUR LOYALTY.
PERHAPS AQUILONIA HAS GAINED A WORTHY SOVEREIGN, AT LAST!
I WILL SEND COUNT TROCERO WORD THAT HE MAY LIFT THE SIEGE.
AND YOU, BARBARIAN--"CONAN," PROSPERO CALLED YOU--WILL YOU SWEAR FEALTY TO ME AS AQUILONIA'S NEW KING?
SINCE I'M CLEARLY NOT GOING TO RULE THIS KINGDOM, WHAT THE HELL DO I CARE WHO DOES?
CONAN...
CAN I COME OUT NOW?
MY LIEGE NUMEDIDES--THIS IS LITTLE ALBIONA--OR, AS PERHAPS I SHOULD NOW REFER TO HER--THE COUNTESS OF MANDIA.
YOU HEAR, CHILD? YOU ARE GOING TO RULE A PROVINCE.
THESE GOOD MEN WILL LOOK OUT FOR YOU.
BUT I NT TO BE TH YOU, CONAN.
NO, YOU DON'T. I'M ONE WHO HAS EVER A HORSE BETWEEN HIS KNEES--OR A BATTLEFIELD OR A SHIP'S DECK BENEATH MY FEET.
BUT PERHAPS--I'LL COME BACK AND VISIT YOU, ONE DAY.
I'LL SEE TO HER, CONAN.

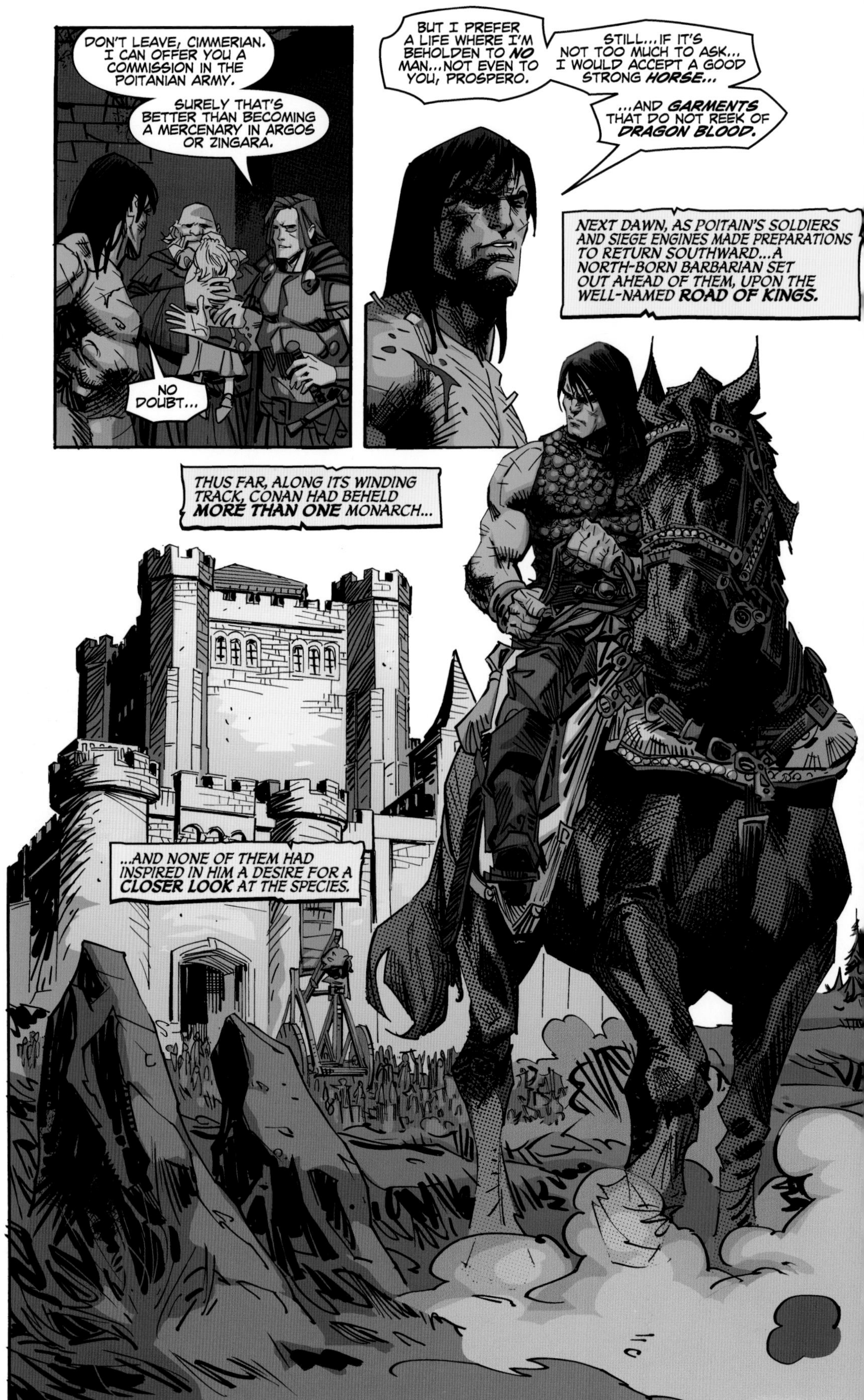
DON'T LEAVE, CIMMERIAN. I CAN OFFER YOU A COMMISSION IN THE POITANIAN ARMY.
SURELY THAT'S BETTER THAN BECOMING A MERCENARY IN ARGOS OR ZINGARA.
NO DOUBT...
BUT I PREFER A LIFE WHERE I'M BEHOLDEN TO NO MAN...NOT EVEN TO YOU, PROSPERO.
STILL...IF IT'S NOT TOO MUCH TO ASK... I WOULD ACCEPT A GOOD STRONG HORSE...
...AND GARMENTS THAT DO NOT REEK OF DRAGON BLOOD.
NEXT DAWN, AS POITAIN'S SOLDIERS AND SIEGE ENGINES MADE PREPARATIONS TO RETURN SOUTHWARD...A NORTH-BORN BARBARIAN SET OUT AHEAD OF THEM, UPON THE WELL-NAMED ROAD OF KINGS.
THUS FAR, ALONG ITS WINDING TRACK, CONAN HAD BEHELD MORE THAN ONE MONARCH...
...AND NONE OF THEM HAD INSPIRED IN HIM A DESIRE FOR A CLOSER LOOK AT THE SPECIES.

CHAPTER FIVE

". . . So things are still touch and go twixt Argos and Zingara . . . and sellswords such as you and I can only hope they give war a chance to flourish."

SOMETIMES THE BEST ROAD...IS A RIVER.
NEAR THE POINT WHERE THE MIGHTY KHOROTAS RIVER, FLOWING SOUTH FROM TARANTIA, WAS JOINED BY THE TRIBUTARY TYBOR, CONAN HAD PURCHASED HIS PASSAGE ON A CATTLE-SCOW BOUND FOR MESSANTIA.
A PAIR OF RANK-AIRED EVENINGS AND MALODOROUS MORNINGS LATER, HOWEVER...

UUUU MUUUUUU

...HE WAS BEGINNING TO **REGRET** THAT DECISION.

Cimmerian in Argos

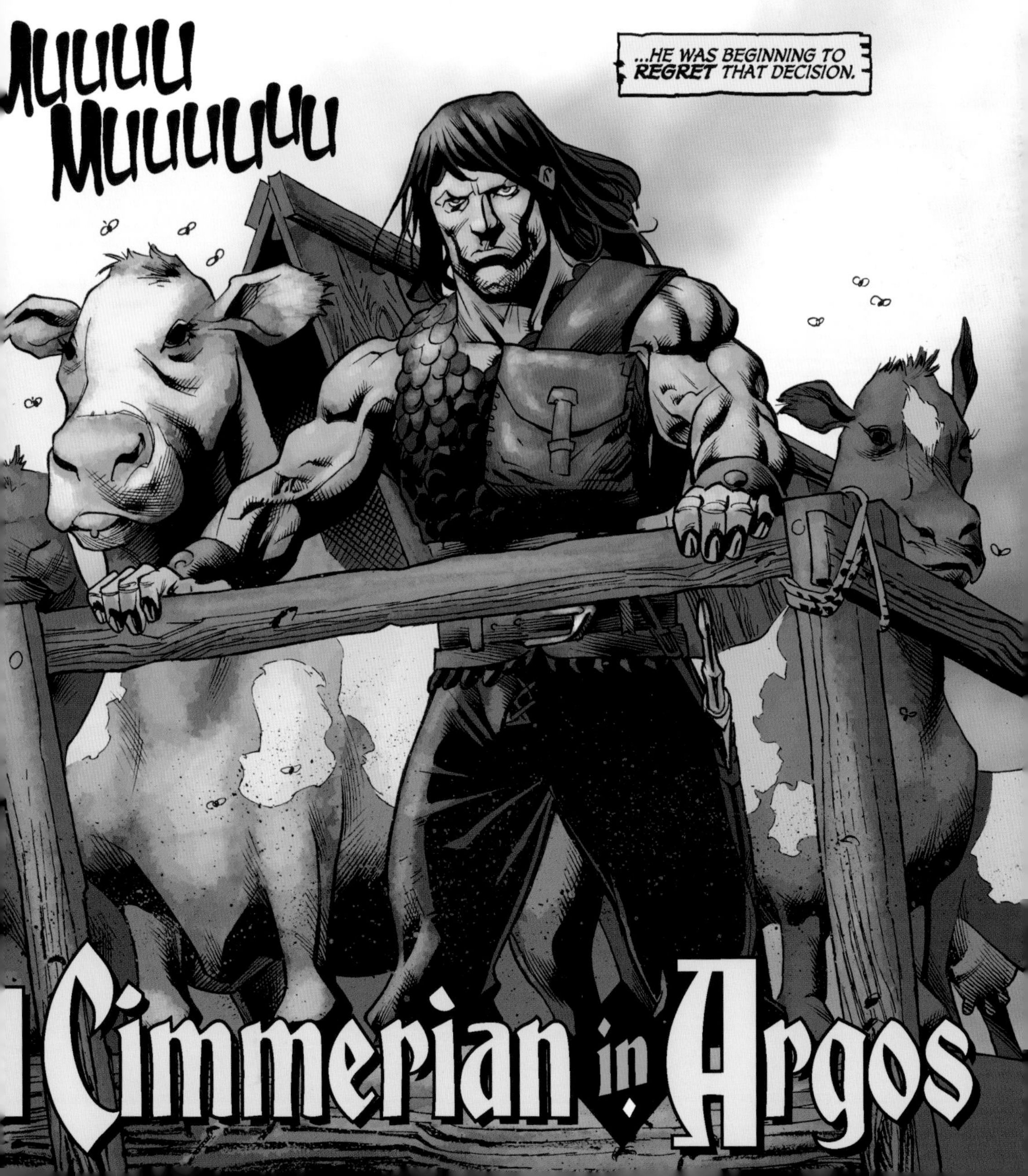

THE VESSEL'S POLE-MEN, INURED TO SUCH PUNGENCIES, HAD OTHER MATTERS ON THEIR VENAL MINDS...
I DON'T LIKE THAT OUTLANDER, WITH HIS FANCY ARMOR AND HIS BARBAROUS ACCENT!
BUT YOU DO LIKE THE LOOK OF THE SADDLEBAGS SLUNG OVER HIS SHOULDER, HEY?
AYE! I HEARD HIM PROMISE OUR SCOW-MASTER SOMETHING GOLD FROM THEM, WHEN WE DOCK AT MESSANTIA.
MMUUUUUUUUUUUUUUUUUUUUU
I'LL WAGER HE DID SOME LOOTING UP IN TARANTIA DURING THE RECENT SIEGE...AND NOW HE'S HOT-FOOTING IT SOUTH TO SET HIMSELF UP IN TRADE IN ARGOS.
EVEN SO, IF YOU WANT TO TRY YOUR LUCK WITH HIM, YOU'RE ON YOUR OWN.
HE'S TOO BIG FOR ME TO TACKLE.
FORGET IT, THEN. I'M NOT TAKING ON A SWORD-WIELDING SAVAGE ALONE...
MMUUUUUUUUUUUUUUUUUUUUU
MY WIFE'S TOO YOUNG TO BE A WIDOW JUST YET.
THE SCOW-DOGS WERE FORTUNATE--FOR THE CIMMERIAN'S KEEN EARS HAD HEARD THEIR SCHEMING EVEN OVER THE CATTLE'S PLAINTS.
LOOK LIVELY, YOU LUBBERS!
CONAN WAS SCOWLING AT THE SWARTHY SCOW-MASTER'S BRASH APPROPRIATION OF THE COLORFUL JARGON OF TRUE SEA-DOGS...
MMUUUUU

WHEN THE REASON FOR HIS
ITBURST CAME INTO VIEW
ROUND A BEND IN THE RIVER.
MESSANTIA, MY SHIPMATES!
SOMEWHERE AHEAD, NOT FAR BEYOND THE FAR-FAMED BRIDGE OF THE SEA'S SORROWS, SPRAWLED THE MYRIAD DOCKS WHERE LAY AT ANCHOR SHIPS THAT PLIED THE WESTERN OCEAN...
BUT THE BARBARIAN'S MIND WAS ON ARGOS ITSELF...AND ON ITS RESTIVE NEIGHBOR ZINGARA.
WILL SOON EACH OUR STINATION, N OF THE NORTH.
O... ELIEVE HAVE METHING R ME?
BY CROM, I'D HAVE RIDDEN INTO ARGOS'S QUEEN PORT IN STYLE, ON THE BACK OF A FINE AQUILONIAN STALLION...
MMUUUU MMUUUU
...IF NOT FOR A VIPER'S BITE NEAR THE POITANIAN BORDER.
THAT'S AS MAY BE. STILL...

AYE, DON'T GET THOSE BULL-HORNS IN AN UPROAR.
I ALWAYS PAY MY PASSAGE, WHETHER IT BE IN STEEL...
...OR IN GOLD.
HMMM...
MMUUUUUUUUUUUUUUUUUUUUUUU
JUST THE ONE PIECE, FROM ALL THOSE YOU MUST HAVE?
PERHAPS IT WOULD BE LESS LONELY WITH A SISTER...
PERHAPS YOU'D BE MORE CIVIL WITH ONE HAND.
ON... SECOND THOUGHT... THIS IS CERTAINLY AMPLE.
MMUUUUUUUUUU
VETTI! ZACCO! ROUST ME WHEN WE'RE APPROACHING THE UNLOADING PENS!
FOR TWO DAYS, CONAN HAD BEEN TEMPTED TO COMMENT ON THE SCOW-MASTER'S HORNED HELMET, WHICH HAD PROBABLY PAID THE FARE OF SOME EARLIER PASSENGER...
BUT HE'D HALF FEARED THE OLD SCOUNDREL WOULD INSIST ON GIVING IT TO HIM.

UPON DOCKING, THE BARBARIAN EAGERLY TOOK HIS LEAVE OF THE SOUNDS AND SMELLS OF THE BARGE...
MMUUUU
IT WAS TASTES HE NOW CRAVED.
SEA-MAN, CAN YOU POINT ME THE WAY TO THE TAVERN OF THE BLACK STAG?
DOWN THREE STREETS...YOU CAN'T MISS IT.
IF YOU SEE ANY OF THE CREW FROM MASTER TITO'S ARGUS IN THERE, REMIND THEM WE SAIL WITH THE MORNING TIDE.
AYE--AND THANKS.
CONAN THREADED HIS WAY WARILY...
FOR THE DARK, CRAMPED ALLEYS OF ANY PORT WERE A GOOD PLACE TO GET ONE'S PURSE STOLEN, AND A THROAT SLIT...
...AS SOMEONE NEAR AT HAND MIGHT WELL HAVE BEEN LEARNING, AT THAT VERY MOMENT...
HAND IT OVER, DOG!
I TOLD YOU JACKALS-- I'VE NAUGHT BUT SWORD AND PLATE-SHIRT.
WE'LL HAVE THEM, THEN!
IN AND AT HIM, BOYS!
THE ROBBERY WAS NONE OF CONAN'S CONCERN... AND THE CORNERED MAN WAS ARMED AND ARMORED...

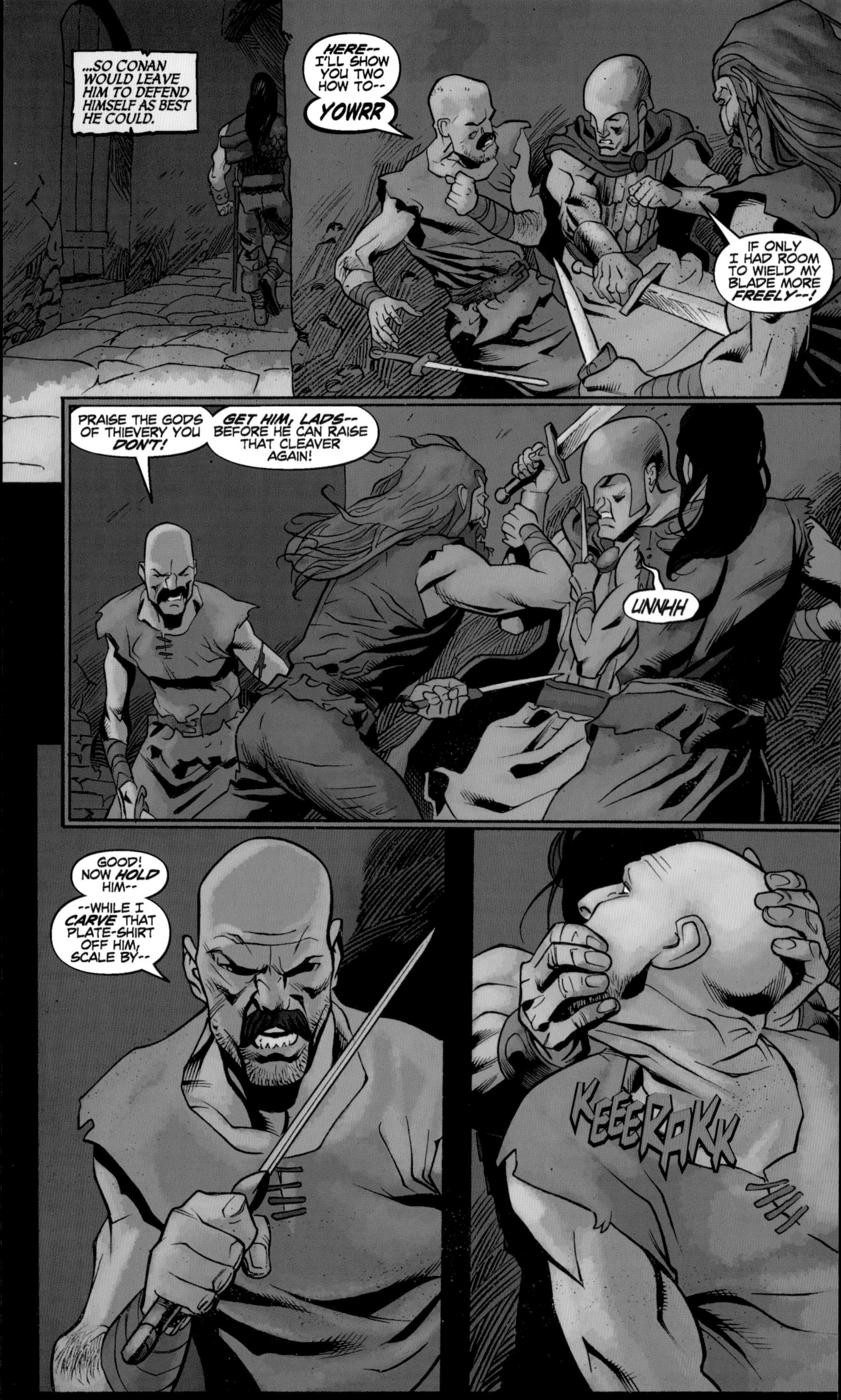
...SO CONAN WOULD LEAVE HIM TO DEFEND HIMSELF AS BEST HE COULD.
HERE-- I'LL SHOW YOU TWO HOW TO--
YOWRR
IF ONLY I HAD ROOM TO WIELD MY BLADE MORE FREELY--!
PRAISE THE GODS OF THIEVERY YOU DON'T!
GET HIM, LADS-- BEFORE HE CAN RAISE THAT CLEAVER AGAIN!
UNNHH
GOOD! NOW HOLD HIM--
--WHILE I CARVE THAT PLATE-SHIRT OFF HIM, SCALE BY--
KEEERAKK

THIS ISN'T YOUR FIGHT, STRANGER.
I DECIDED IT WAS NO FAIR ONE, EITHER.
LOOK AT HIM, MAN! HIS ARMOR WILL FETCH A FEW LYRKA AT PUBLIO'S, AS WELL!
FOR A FLEETING MOMENT, CONAN CONSIDERED WARNING THE TWO REMAINING ROBBERS OFF.
BUT, ON THE INSTANT, HE REALIZED IT WOULD FALL ON DEAF EARS...
HE DID WHAT CAME
NATURALLY TO HIM.
URRGGK
GHAAAA
SLASSSH
WHY DID YOU INTERFERE, CONAN? I HAD THE BATTLE WELL IN HAND.
EH? HOW DID YOU KNOW MY--
PERHAPS IF I BARE MY HEAD LIKE YOURS...
IVANOS!

I THOUGHT YOU WERE PUSHING UP DOLPHINS FROM THE BOTTOM OF THE VILAYET, WITH AN ARROW IN YOUR BREASTBONE!
I HAD SIMILAR THOUGHTS ABOUT YOU--
--AFTER I SAW YOU GO OVER THE SIDE OF THE OLIVIA WITH FOUR TURANIANS CLINGING TO YOU LIKE BARNACLES!
IT SEEMS WE WERE BOTH LUCKY.
BUT WHAT OF OUR SHIPMATES?
KRIMSAR, FOR INSTANCE--OR THE FAIR OLIVIA HERSELF?
AS IT HAPPENED, WE THREE WOUND UP ON SOME SHORE TOGETHER--
AND, IN TIME, I RESTORED OLIVIA TO...HER FATHER'S HOUSE.
AND KRIMSAR, THAT LOVABLE ZAMORIAN WEASEL?
WE TOOK A TURN THIEVING TOGETHER IN SHADIZAR THE WICKED...
...BEFORE HE WAS MURDERED... BY AN ASSASSIN WITH A SWORD FOR AN ARM.
KRIMSAR'S KILLER AND I MET UP AGAIN IN THE GOLDEN HILLS OF OPHIR...
AND YOU'RE HE WHICH ME HIS ASSA NOW PL HIS TRA IN HEL
COME. I TAKE IT YOU WERE ON YOUR WAY TO THAT TAVERN I'D TOLD YOU ABOUT.
WE'LL DRINK A TOAST THERE TO POOR KRIMSAR...
...AND TO THE OH-SO-BEAUTIFUL OLIVIA WHO CERTAINLY DESERVED TO ENTERTAIN BETTE THAN PIRATES IN HER BED.
PRESENT COMPANY ALWAY EXCEPTED, OF COURSE.

A SHORT WALK LATER...
...SO THINGS ARE STILL TOUCH AND GO TWIXT ARGOS AND ZINGARA...
...AND SELL-SWORDS SUCH AS YOU AND I CAN ONLY HOPE THEY GIVE WAR A CHANCE TO FLOURISH.
AH... HERE WE ARE...
I THINK YOU'LL LIKE THIS PLACE.

CAPTAIN HERMIAS--!

I'VE ASKED YOU BEFORE NOT TO DO THAT!
I HAVE A MAN-FRIEND...
THEN YOU SHOULD BE WELL USED TO HAVING YOUR RUMP PATTED, LASS!

CAN I HELP YOU TWO BIG, STRONG WARRIORS?
IF SHE'S THE FACE--AND OTHER PARTS--OF THIS TAVERN, I LIKE IT ALREADY.
EASY, CIMMERIAN. SHE'S--

OH. NOW I SEE.
SORRY. I DIDN'T KNOW SHE WAS TAKEN.

IVANOS AND I HAVE NO QUARREL WITH THE ROAMING EYE OF THE CAPTAIN OF THE GUARDS, STRANGER--ONLY WITH HIS WANDERING HANDS.
SHANDI, THIS IS THE FAMOUS CONAN I'VE TOLD YOU ABOUT--
--THE BEST PIRATE CAPTAIN I EVER SAILED WITH!
SINCE THE ONLY OTHER ONE YOU SAILED UNDER WAS SERGIUS OF KHROSHA, IT WAS NOT MUCH OF A CONTEST.

SHANDI'S A GOOD LASS, CONAN. WE PLAN TO WED WHEN MY BONUS AS A SOLDIER IN THE ARGOSSEAN ARMY COMES THROUGH.
THEN ARGOS IS STILL HIRING MERCENARIES, IN CASE WAR COMES?

OH, THEY STILL NEED A FEW GOOD MEN...
BUT YOU'LL NEED TO ADD TO YOUR ARMOR, IF YOU WANT TO BE TAKEN FOR ANYTHING OTHER THAN SPEAR FODDER.

YOUR SIGNING BONUS SHOULD COVER THE COST, BUT THEY WON'T PAY IN ADVANCE.
I'VE STILL A FEW GOLD TRINKETS THAT SHOULD SEE TO MY NEEDS.

GOOD! I'LL SEND YOU TO SOMEONE WHO WILL FIT YOU UP!
AH! I SEE YOU'RE ADMIRING MORE OF THE LOCAL SCENERY.

I'LL HAVE SHANDI ASK DARA TO JOIN US LATER--BUT NOW WE MUST GO OUR SEPARATE WAYS.

MEET ME BACK HERE AFTER DARK...

...AND WE ONE-TIME PIRATES WILL CAROUSE LIKE THE SUN'S STILL ON THE YARDARM!

CONAN RETURNED TO THE DOCKS THE WAY HE HAD COME.
HE NOTED THAT NO ONE HAD YET CLEARED THE ALLEYS OF THE THREE CORPSES HE HAD LEFT THERE.

PUT YOUR BACKS INTO THAT SCRUBBING, YOU WATER LILIES!
THE CIMMERIAN BARELY GLANCED AT THE ARGUS, OF WHOSE CREWMAN HE HAD ASKED DIRECTIONS EARLIER.
HE'D HAD ENOUGH OF SAILING ON THE VILAYET SEA TO LAST HIM FOR A LIFETIME.

AT LENGTH, AS IVANOS HAD SAID, A SIGN THAT BORE NO SYMBOL FLUTTERED SLIGHTLY IN THE BREEZE FROM THE SEA.
A FITTING "NAME," CONAN THOUGHT, FOR A BUSINESS RUN BY A MAN WHO DEALT IN EVERYTHING--
--AND IN NOTHING THAT COULD BE TRACED TO ITS RIGHTFUL OWNER.
YOU ARE PUBLIO?
I AM.
I'VE HEARD YOUR NAME SPOKEN TWICE SINCE I ARRIVED IN TOWN THIS MORNING... ONCE BY A GOOD SOLDIER...ONCE BY A MURDEROUS CUTPURSE.
ONE MUST TRAVEL IN ALL KINDS OF CIRCLES IN A PORT CITY, OUTLANDER.
WHAT DO YOU WANT...?

...THOUGH, I WARN YOU, I DO NOT TRADE MY VALUABLE WARES FOR SHRUNKEN HEADS OR STRINGS OF BEADS OR...

ON THE OTHER HAND...IT IS ALWAYS A PLEASURE TO DEAL WITH A MAN OF QUALITY.
KLUNK

LOOK AROUND! PRIZES FROM THE WORLD OVER WASH UP ON MY FABLED SHORES.
I'M SURE THEY DO.

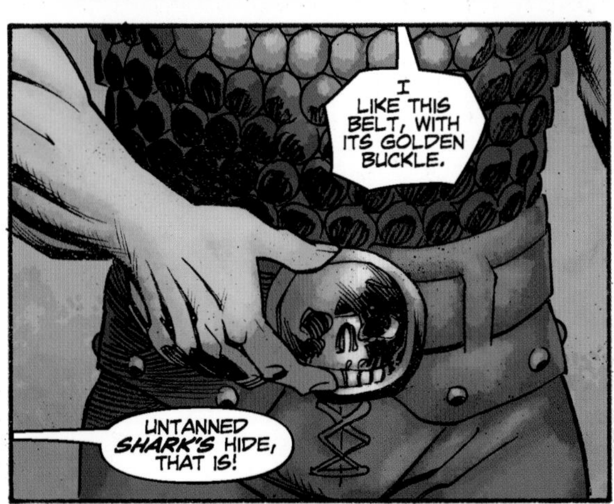
I LIKE THIS BELT, WITH ITS GOLDEN BUCKLE.
UNTANNED SHARK'S HIDE, THAT IS!

ALSO THESE...

...AND THESE!
SUITS YOU, SIRRAH!

AND THAT.
LET ME SHOW YOU SOMETHING MORE PRACTICAL.
THOSE HORNS CAN SWING LOOSE IN BATTLE AND PUT OUT AN EYE...

I'LL TAKE IT.
PERHAPS THAT SCOW-MASTER HAD KNOWN SOMETHING, AFTER ALL.

OH, AND THAT--
--AND I'LL BE ON MY WAY.
OH, YES--NOTHING LIKE A FINE SCARLET CLOAK TO ADD THE PROPER MARTIAL TOUCH BENEATH THAT WARLIKE HELMET...
YOU THINK TO MOCK ME SLYLY, ARGOSSEAN.
I WOULD ADVISE YOU TO STOP DOING SO.
I ASSURE YOU, YOU MISINTERPRET MY MEANING, GOOD SIR.
NOW, AS TO THE MINOR MATTER OF PAYMENT...
WILL THIS COVER EVERYTHING?
WHY, AS A MATTER OF FACT, IT WILL--
--JUST BARELY.

IT'S TIME I WAS GOING...WHILE I'VE STILL A FEW COINS LEFT IN MY BOOT.

IF YOU PLEASE...

THERE IS STILL **ONE MORE** ITEM IN MY **BACK ROOM** THAT I WOULD HAVE YOU SEE.

ALL RIGHT... BUT SHOW ME QUICKLY.

IT WILL NOT TAKE LONG, I ASSURE YOU.

I SEE NOTHING OF INTEREST HERE.

JUST WAIT RIGHT THERE...

DID YOU REALLY THINK A NORTHERN BARBARIAN WOULDN'T KNOW A *TRAPDOOR* BENEATH HIS HEELS WHEN HE STEPPED ON ONE?

THOUGH, CLEARLY, THERE *HAVE* BEEN ONE OR TWO WHO FELL FOR YOUR LITTLE TRICK.

YOU WOULD HAVE HAD TO SCRAMBLE DOWN TO RETRIEVE YOUR COINAGE, BUT YOU FELT IT WAS WORTH THE TROUBLE.

NOW TELL ME, PUBLIO--AND IN A VERY FEW WORDS--

--WHY I SHOULD N IMPALE YOU THOSE DEA "FANGS" BELOW!

B-BECAUSE--IF YOU *SPARE* ME--YOU CAN KEEP ALL YOU FOUND IN MY SHOP FOR ***NO PAYMENT!***

I WOULD DO THAT ANYWAY.

AND I'LL PAY YOU THE ***SAME*** SUM AGAIN!

HE ***LIKED*** *DOING BUSINESS WITH PUBLIO, CONAN DECIDED.*

HE WOULD HAVE TO DO IT ***AGAIN*** *SOMETIME.*

BUT, RIGHT THEN, HE FELT LIKE A ***DRINK*** *OR THREE...BEFORE HE RETURNED TO THE BLACK STAG FOR SOME* ***SERIOUS*** *IMBIBING.*

AS IT HAPPENED--HIS OWN BUSINESS FINISHED EARLY--IVANOS ARRIVED BACK AT THE BLACK STAG JUST AT DUSK.
HO, SHANDI.
IVANOS! A SIGHT FOR EYES WEARY FROM LOOKING ON DRUNKEN SOTS.
YOU MUST BE LOSING YOUR TOUCH, CAPTAIN HERMIAS!
SHUT YOUR TEETH, TORIO!
I COLLECTED A EBT OWED ME. WHERE WOULD OU LIKE TO GO WHEN YOU GET OFF WORK?
ANYWHERE BUT HERE! THOSE LOUTS HAVE BEEN DRINKING SINCE MORNING...
YOU ARROGANT LITTLE SLUT--
SPURNING A CAPTAIN OF THE GUARDS--FOR SOME LOW-LIFE MERCENARY!
LET ME GO!
GET YOUR HANDS OFF HER--NOW!
WHAT MY HANDS DO TO HER HAD BEST BE NONE OF YOUR BUSINESS--
--UNLESS YOU WANT TO WIND UP IN THE KING'S DUNGEON!
COME ON, YOU!
I SAID RELEASE HER--

--NOW!
IVANOS-- NO!
BY MITRA, I'LL CUT OUT YOUR GIZZARD AND FEED IT TO MY HOUND!

FEED HIM YOUR OWN!
HGGKKK

Y-YOU... YOU'VVVVV...
YES. IT SEEMS I HAVE.

YOU MURDERED HIM, YOU CORINTHIAN SCUM!
I ONLY GAVE HIM WHAT HE MEANT TO GIVE ME!
AND FOR IT, WE'LL SLICE O YOUR SWORD ARM--AND CL YOU TO DEAT WITH IT!

THE DEVIL YOU WILL!

HURRY, SHANDI! THEY'D TREAT YOU NO BETTER!
WE MUST LIE LOW, TILL ALL THIS DIES DOWN!

SO IT WAS THAT, SOON AFTER DARK, CONAN ARRIVED---HALF-INTOXICATED AND FULLY IN GOOD HUMOR...
THAT'S HIM!
THAT'S THE ONE WHO WAS WITH THE CORINTHIAN!
IVANOS? SO WHAT IF I WAS?
WHERE IS HE?
COWERING IN SOME DARK CORNER OF HELL, MOST LIKE--EH, LT. TORIO?
YOUR FRIEND KILLED CAPTAIN HERMIAS--SO TELL US WHERE HE'S RUN TO, WHILE YOU'VE STILL GOT A TONGUE IN YOUR HEAD!
I WOULD NOT TELL YOU WHERE IVANOS WAS, EVEN IF I KNEW.
THEN WE'LL TAKE YOU SOMEPLACE QUIET--WHERE YOU CAN SCREAM OUT HIS HIDING-PLACE WITH YOUR FINAL BREATH!
REMOVE YOUR SWORD-BELT--SLOWLY--WITH YOUR LEFT HAND.
AND WE'LL TAKE THOSE SADDLEBAGS YOU KEEP SO CLOSE TO YOUR HEART...

YOU...WANT MY SADDLEBAGS?
VERY WELL, THEN...
TAKE THEM!
HNNNFF
GOLD! LOOK-- GOLD!
IT'S SPILLING FRO HIS SACKS!
I SAW THIS BRACELET FIRST!
THIS IS MINE--AND THIS-- AND--
OUT OF OUR WAY, DOGS!

EVEN IN HIS INEBRIATED STATE, CONAN KNEW IT WAS WISER TO FLEE THAN TO FIGHT MEN WHO WERE IN THE EMPLOY OF ARGOS'S KING...
YET, THE ERRANT FATES SEEMED TO HAVE CONSPIRED AGAINST HIM...
THERE'S THE MATE TO MY BRACELET!
OOOPH! WATCH WHERE YOU'RE GOING!
THE ROOM SPUN BEFORE CONAN'S EYES LIKE A DRUNKEN DERVISH.
STILL, HE MADE TO RETRIEVE HIS NEW HELMET BEFORE HE--
THRAKKK

YOU-- KILLED HIM!
WOULD THAT I HAD! HE'S STILL BREATHING...
HE MUST HAVE A HEAD HARDER THAN A TAXMAN'S HEART!
HEAR ME! I AM CONFISCATING ALL THIS CRIMINAL'S GOLD IN THE NAME OF THE KING--
AND ANYONE WHO TRIES TO HOLD BACK ENOUGH TO MAKE A TOOTH WILL WISH HIS MOTHER HAD STRANGLED HIM AT BIRTH!
DO I MAKE MYSELF--
--CLEAR?
KLK
KLANK
KKK
I CONGRATULATE YOU ALL, FOR THE FAITHFUL SUBJECTS OF HIS MAJESTY THAT YOU ARE.
NOW GO BACK TO YOUR DRINKING.
AS FOR THIS FOOL BARBARIAN-- HE HAS A DATE WITH JUDGE MACABRUS IN THE MORNING--
--AND DOUBTLESS WITH THE EXECUTIONER, COME THE AFTERNOON!

CHAPTER SIX

"There's nothing I want that you can give me, dog . . .
My freedom is mine—for the taking!"

...AND FINALLY, AWASH ONLY IN THE FRIGID FILTH FLUNG FROM AN EMPTIED SLOPBUCKET.

RRRRRR

IS IT A MAN WE HAVE AWAKENED, LADS--

--OR SOME SNARLING JUNGLE BEAST?

CONAN'S DAY IN COURT

PERHAPS IT'S SOMETHING IN BETWEEN THE TWO, LT. TORIO.
ADDRESS ME AS YOUR CAPTAIN, SOLDIER--
FOR I'LL BE PROMOTED, FOR SURE, ONCE MY SUPERIORS LEARN I BROUGHT IN HERMIAS'S MURDERER.
I'LL PROMOTE YOU--RIGHT UP THE DEVIL'S BACKSIDE--
--IF YOU'RE THE ONE WHO STRUCK ME DOWN FROM BEHIND!
I DID--AND YOU MUST HAVE A HEAD MADE OF ROCK.
ELSE YOUR SKULL WOULD NOW BE AS SPLINTERED AS THE BENCH I HIT YOU WITH!
YOU COWARDLY SON OF A SHE-CUR--!
HGGGK

DID YOU REALLY THINK I'D STAND SO NEAR A WILD ANIMAL-- UNLESS IT WAS SECURED BY IRON?
AHH...I CAN SEE IT'S ALL COMING BACK TO YOU NOW...
THE FIGHT IN THE BLACK STAG... WHICH ENDED UP WITH YOU FACE DOWN ON THE FLOOR-PLANKS.
IF YOU THINK STICKING ME IN THIS STINKING CELL WILL MAKE ME TELL YOU WHERE IVANOS AND HIS GIRL HAVE FLED--
OH, I BELIEVE YOU WHEN YOU SAY YOU DON'T KNOW.
BUT THINGS HAVE GONE BEYOND THAT NOW.
YOU'RE SET TO STAND TRIAL-- AND, NO DOUBT, SENTENCING-- TOMORROW AT DAWN.
NO, MAKE THAT TODAY, FOR IT'S PAST THE MIDNIGHT HOUR.
FEAR NOT. I'LL FIND IVANOS ON MY OWN--
AND I'LL RELISH HIS SCREAMS BEFORE I LET HIM DIE--

--*AFTER* I'VE SHOWN HIS *SLUT* WHAT IT'S LIKE TO BE MOUNTED BY A *REAL* MAN!

HA HA HA HA HA HA HA HA HA HA HA HA HA

PTUUUI

URRGG

YOU--A MERE TURNKEY--WOULD THWART THE WILL OF AN OFFICER OF THE KING'S GUARDS?
I WOULD NEVER DARE TO DO SO...

...BUT YOU AND I BOTH KNOW JUDGE MACABRUS WOULD TAKE IT AMISS IF A PRISONER WERE SLAUGHTERED IN HIS CELL--THE NIGHT BEFORE HE WAS DUE TO STAND BEFORE HIM IN THE DOCK.

OR ARE YOU EAGER TO HAVE HIM PASS HIS USUAL SENTENCE ON YOU, AS WELL?
ALL RIGHT... ALL RIGHT! I'LL LEAVE HIM TO THE JUDGE'S TENDER MERCIES.

BUT I SWEAR TO YOU, IF HE DECIDES TO LET THE BARBARIAN GO--

--I'LL DEAL WITH THE DOG, THE MOMENT HE SETS FOOT OUTSIDE!

HEY, TORIO!

WHY DON'T YOU GIVE ME YOUR SWORD--SINCE YOU SEEM SO RELUCTANT TO USE IT?

MOTHER OF MITRA, I'LL--

C-CAREFUL, LIEUTENANT! REMEMBER MACABRUS!

THEN SHUT THAT DOOR--BEFORE I BATHE MY BLADE IN RED!

SLAAMM
YOU THERE IN THE SHADOWS-- STEP FORWARD!
THEY'RE GONE--AND WOULD SEE W WAS SPYING UPON US.
NOT SPYING, BOY. OLD SOLONUS DOESN'T SPY.
BUT I DID NOT THINK TH GUARDSMA WANTED A WITNESS.
...NOT EVEN ONE WHO'LL PROBABLY NEVER AGAIN SEE ANYTHING SAVE BY TORCHLIGHT.
MY CELLMATE, THEN...AT LEAST FOR THIS ONE NIGHT.
WHAT ARE YOU IMPRISONED FOR, OLD MAN?
I HAVE BEEN HERE SO LONG, I SWEAR I HAVE FORGOTTEN.
I THINK IT MAY HAVE INVOLVED A YOUNG GIRL... OR ELSE A GOAT... OR PERHAPS A YOUNG GIRL AND A GOAT.

AT LEAST I'M GLAD I NEVER CAME BEFORE "OLD GALLOWS-BREATH."
THE JUDGE THEY SPOKE OF?
AYE. HE MAY LET A MAN STEW A WHILE FIRST IN HIS CELL--
--OR TURN HIM OVER AT ONCE TO THE COURT TORTURER--
--BUT, IN THE END, HE HANGS EVERYONE WHO COMES BEFORE HIM.
AND NOT ALWAYS BY THEIR NECK.
NO ONE HAS EVER WALKED FREE AT THE HAND OF THIS JUDGE.
THEN THERE IS NO SENSE IN TROUBLING MYSELF...
...CONCERNING AN OUTCOME THAT NOTHING SHORT OF AN ACT OF THE GODS WILL CHANGE.
SNOORRRRR

A FEW HOURS LATER...
THAT'S THE ONE, HIGH CONSTABLE!
STAND UP, DOG!
I SAID STAND UP, OR I'LL SLICE OFF YOUR LEGS SO YOU CAN'T STAND!
NO, YOU WON'T. IT'S FOR JUDGE MACABRUS TO DECIDE IF HE IS GUILTY--OR INNOCENT.
HAHAHAHAHA
UNCHAIN THE OUTLANDER, THE QUICKER TO DRAG HIM INTO COURT.
THE JUDGE WANTS TO GET HIS TRIAL OUT OF THE WAY BEFORE DAYBREAK...
...SO HE CAN ATTEND A CONT IN WHICH ONE OF GLADIATORS COMPETING

THERE! YOU'RE *FREE*-- IN A MANNER OF SPEAKING.
YOU TWO-- BRING HIM *ALONG!*
YOU NEED NOT LAY HANDS ON ME.

I SAID--

KEEP YOUR *HANDS* OFF ME!
THOK
THUK

CAPTAIN-- LET US *GUT* THAT--
I'LL COME WITH YOU, TORIO-- FOR THERE'S NO SENSE IN TRYING TO ESCAPE--
--BUT I'LL NOT HAVE THESE VERMIN TOUCH ME.
KEEP IN *FRONT* OF ME, THEN--AND MAKE NO SUDDEN MOVES!

THEY CALLED YOU *"CAPTAIN."*
I HAVE EEN OFFICIALLY APPOINTED TO PLACE THE MAN YOUR FRIEND SLEW.

SO, IN THE END, HE DID ME A *FAVOR.*
PERHAPS LATER I'LL DO *YOU* ONE--IF THEY'LL LET ME PLAY *HANGMAN,* JUST THIS ONCE!

THE COURTROOM, CONAN SURMISED, WAS LOCATED DIRECTLY ABOVE THE DANK CELLS OF THE ROYAL DUNGEON...
HMM... PERHAPS THE JUDGE HAS THOUGHT BETTER OF HOLDING A TRIAL AT DAWN.
I HOPE HE SHOWS UP SOON!
...IT CLEARLY BEING HELD PRUDENT AND EFFICIENT IN MESSANTIA TO DISPENSE ALL THE STAGES OF JUSTICE BENEATH ONE ROOF.
I'VE LEFT MY HORSE TETHERED OUTSIDE, SO I CAN MAKE FOR THE GLADIATORIAL GAMES MYSELF, AS SOON AS--
KREEEEKK
ALL HONOR TO JUDGE MACABRUS!
SILENCE MY COU
STAND UP STRAIGHTER, HEATHEN!
GET THAT PIG-STICKER OUT OF MY BACK!
HIGH CONSTABLE-- WHAT IS THE CHARGE AGAINST THIS UNKEMPT PRISONER I SEE BEFORE ME?

I DEFER TO
APTAIN TORIO
OF THE KING'S
GUARDS.
MILORD, LAST NIGHT, A SOLDIER ACCOMPLICE OF THIS NORTHRON KILLED MY LATE SUPERIOR FOR NO REASON--
--AND THIS DOG
EFUSES TO DIVULGE
ERE THE MURDERER
HAS RUN OFF TO!
MORE: TWO OF MY MEN WERE WOUNDED IN BRINGING HIM IN FOR QUESTIONING.
INDEED? BUT HE'S A HALF-NAKED SAVAGE...
...AND SURELY YOU AND YOUR MEN WORE ARMOR...
HE WAS NOT THEN ACCOUTERED AS HE IS NOW, MILORD.
LAST NIGHT, IN MAWKISH IMITATION OF HIS CIVILIZED BETTERS--
--HE WORE ALL THIS GARB!
I, OF COURSE, HAVE CONFISCATED HIS SWORD, BY RIGHT OF BEING THE ARRESTING OFFICER.
THIS ARMOR LOOKS TO BE OF SOME QUALITY... STOLEN, NO DOUBT.
I'LL HAVE IT, TO DEFRAY COURT COSTS...AND THAT INCLUDES THE SWORD, CAPTAIN.
STILL, ARGOS IS NOW SHORT ONE DESERTED SOLDIER--
--AND, WITH THIS DAMNED WAR LOOMING WITH ZINGARA, IT COULD USE A REPLACEMENT WARRIOR OF THIS ONE'S BULK...

SO, PRISONER--
GIVEN OUR PERILOUS TIMES, AND AGAINST MY USUAL PRACTICE...
...I WILL DELIVER YOU UP, IF ARMORLESS, INTO THE RANKS OF OUR ARMY...
...IF YOU'LL MERELY TELL US WHE YOUR COMPANION H GONE, SO HE MAY B APPREHENDED.
SURELY THE JUDGE DOESN'T MEAN TO SPARE THE SAVAGE!
HE IS LYING, TO ELICIT THE TRUTH--AT LEAST, I HOPE HE IS!
WELL, BARBARIAN?...
WHERE IS YOUR MURDEROUS FRIEND HIDING?
AS YOU SAY--HE IS A FRIEND OF MINE--
--SO I CANNOT BETRAY HIM.
HEAR ME, FELLOW! IT IS YOUR DUTY TO THE STATE TO REVEAL WHAT YOU KNOW OF YOUR COMRADE'S WHEREABOUTS!
MY DUTY? TO WHAT STATE?
TO ARGOS, OF COURSE!
BUT I AM NOT AN ARGOSSEAN... AND THUS OWE NOTHING TO THIS KINGDOM OR ITS RULER.
I AM CONAN... A CIMMERIAN.

WHAT?! WILL YOU SPURN MY GENEROUS OFFER--
--OF LIFE, WHEN I WAS SORELY TEMPTED TO DEAL OUT DEATH?
ARE YOU DETERMINED TO DANCE ON THE END OF A GALLOWS ROPE?
YOUR SILENCE REVEALS YOU TO STAND IN CONTEMPT OF THIS HIGH COURT!
VERY WELL, THEN! I'LL NOT HANG YOU STRAIGHT AWAY.
BUT I SENTENCE YOU TO BE THROWN BACK INTO THE DUNGEON--
--TO ROT, IN BETWEEN VISITS WITH THE ROYAL TORTURER--
--UNTIL YOU REVEAL YOUR FRIEND'S WHEREABOUTS!
DO YOU SEE, NOW, WHAT YOU HAVE COME TO?
I SEE...
...THAT YOU ARE ALL MAD.

--SO I'LL TARRY HERE NO LONGER!
STOP HIM!
THRAK
UHRRR
I'LL HAVE MY SWORD, TORIO--
HMMFF
AND, SINCE YOU WANTED IT, AS WELL, JUDGE--
--SO WILL YOU!
SPLUNTCH
GRRGGGL

YOU BLOOD-THIRSTING DOG! I'LL--
I DON'T CRAVE BLOOD--

BUT I DRINK DEEP FROM ITS CUP WHEN I MUST!
NNNGG

HERE, TORIO--

--ANOTHER CORPSE FOR YOUR NEW COMMAND!

I'LL HAVE MY MAIL-SHIRT BACK--

--SO I NO LONGER LOOK LIKE A "HALF-NAKED SAVAGE"!

HAH!
KLANGK
OOMPH
THEY MUST HAVE NAMED YOU HIGH CONSTABLE--
--BECAUSE YOU CLEARLY HAVE NO TALENT FOR LOWERING YOURSELF TO SWORDPLAY!
K-KEEP BACK...
BUT YOU DID FORBID TORIO TO CUT OFF MY LEGS...
...SO I'LL LEAVE YOU YOUR LIFE--AND YOUR SWORD-ARM INTACT--
YYAAAAA
--THE BETTER TO PRACTICE WITH.

ON YOUR FEET AGAIN, TORIO?
YOU WANTED MY SWORD... SO TAKE IT.
I HAVE THE CONSTABLE'S.

CAPTAIN! WE'LL CATCH HIM BETWEEN US!
A GOOD ENOUGH PLAN--

--IF THE KING DID NOT EMPLOY GUARDS FIT ONLY FOR BULLYING SERVING-GIRLS!
GGGG
SPLANGK
HUNNH

NOW, TORIO-- IT'S DOWN TO YOU AND ME.
YOU-- MIGHT KILL ME-- OR I MIGHT KILL YOU--

BUT ALL YOU REALLY WANT--IS TO FLEE THIS PLACE, BEFORE MORE GUARDS ARRIVE.
AND I SEE THAT ONLY I STAND BETWEEN YOU AND THE OPEN DOORWAY.

SO--LOOK! I'M STEPPING ASIDE!
THE WAY OUT NOW YAWNS WIDE BEFORE YOU!

DON'T WASTE TIME STRAPPING ON YOUR STUPID GREAVES!

THERE'S NOTHING I WANT THAT YOU CAN GIVE ME, DOG...

KTANGG
MY FREEDOM IS MINE--FOR THE TAKING!

RUN, DAMN YOU! CAN'T YOU HEAR THEM?
ARMED MEN-- RUNNING THIS WAY!
SPLANGG
YOU LIE! I'D HEAR THEIR THUMPING BOOTS LONG BEFORE YOU WOULD!
BY MITRA, I'M ALL THROUGH ACTING OUT OF FEAR!
GGGAAAAA

YOUR LOSS OF FEAR, DOG--
GGGGHH...
--WAS YOUR FINAL MISTAKE!
AS CONAN FASTENED HIS FALLEN CLOAK, HE SEEMED TO RECALL...
HADN'T THE HIGH CONSTABLE SAID SOMETHING ABOUT LEAVING HIS HORSE OUTSIDE?

WHO THE DEVIL--?
CLOSE ENOUGH!
THOK
AT LAST, THOSE OTHER GUARDS THAT TORIO HAD DESPERATELY IMAGINED HEARING WERE ACTUALLY COMING, ON THE RUN.
CONAN DID NOT KNOW MESSANTIA, AND WAS LIKELY TO QUICKLY RUN HIMSELF INTO A CUL-DE-SAC, WHILE THE TWO BEHIND HIM WERE JOINED BY TWENTY MORE.
THUS, AT THIS FARTHEST END OF THE ROAD OF KINGS HE HAD TRAVELED...
...THERE WAS, AT LONG LAST, ONLY ONE MORE ROAD TRULY OPEN TO HIM NOW...

THE GREAT AND FORBIDDING WESTERN OCEAN--
--AND THE UNGLIMPSED LANDS TO WHICH IT LED!

THE WORLDS OF ROBERT E. HOWARD

Dark Horse is proud to continue our tradition of bringing Robert E. Howard's incomparable characters to life!

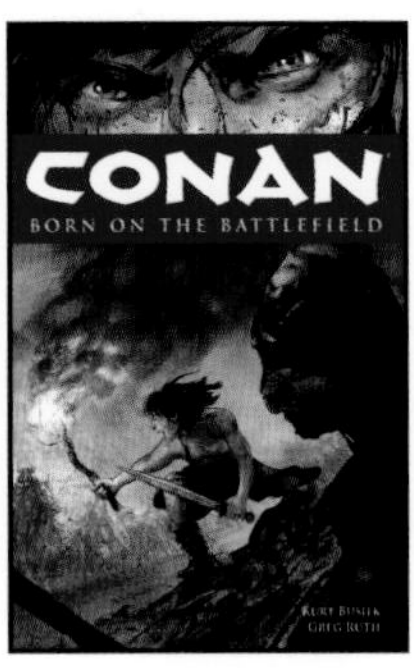

CONAN®

THE CHRONICLES OF CONAN

Roy Thomas, Barry Windsor-Smith, Gil Kane, John Buscema, Neal Adams, Howard Chaykin, and others

Volume 1: Tower of the Elephant and Other Stories
ISBN 978-1-59307-016-8 | $15.99

Volume 2: Rogues in the House and Other Stories
ISBN 978-1-59307-023-6 | $16.99

Volume 3: The Monster of the Monoliths and Other Stories
ISBN 978-1-59307-024-3 | $15.99

Volume 4: The Song of Red Sonja and Other Stories
ISBN 978-1-59307-025-0 | $15.99

Volume 5: The Shadow in the Tomb and Other Stories
ISBN 978-1-59307-175-2 | $15.99

Volume 6: The Curse of the Golden Skull and Other Stories
ISBN 978-1-59307-274-2 | $15.99

Volume 7: The Dweller in the Pool and Other Stories
ISBN 978-1-59307-300-8 | $15.99

Volume 8: Brothers of the Blade and Other Stories
ISBN 978-1-59307-349-7 | $16.99

Volume 9: Riders of the River-Dragons and Other Stories
ISBN 978-1-59307-394-7 | $16.99

Volume 10: When Giants Walk the Earth and Other Stories
ISBN 978-1-59307-490-6 | $16.99

Volume 11: The Dance of the Skull and Other Stories
ISBN 978-1-59307-636-8 | $16.99

Volume 12: The Beast King of Abombi and Other Stories
ISBN 978-1-59307-778-5 | $16.99

Volume 13: Whispering Shadows and Other Stories
ISBN 978-1-59307-837-9 | $16.99

Volume 14: Shadow of the Beast and Other Stories
ISBN 978-1-59307-899-7 | $16.99

Volume 15: The Corridor of Mullah-Kajar and Other Stories
ISBN 978-1-59307-971-0 | $16.99

Volume 16: The Eternity War and Other Stories
ISBN 978-1-59582-176-8 | $16.99

Volume 17: The Creation Quest and Other Stories
ISBN 978-1-59582-177-5 | $17.99

Volume 18: Isle of the Dead and Other Stories
ISBN 978-1-59582-382-3 | $17.99

Volume 19: Deathmark and Other Stories
ISBN 978-1-59582-515-5 | $17.99

Volume 20: Night of the Wolf and Other Stories
ISBN 978-1-59582-584-1 | $18.99

Volume 21: Blood of the Titan and Other Stories
ISBN 978-1-59582-704-3 | $18.99

CONAN MINISERIES

Conan and the Jewels of Gwahlur
P. Craig Russell
ISBN 978-1-59307-491-3 | $13.99

Conan and the Demons of Khitai
Akira Yoshida and Paul Lee
ISBN 978-1-59307-543-9 | $12.99

Conan: Book of Thoth
Kurt Busiek, Len Wein, and Kelley Jones
ISBN 978-1-59307-648-1 | $17.99

Conan and the Songs of the Dead
Joe R. Lansdale and Tim Truman
ISBN 978-1-59307-718-1 | $14.99

Conan and the Midnight God
Josh Dysart, Will Conrad, and Jason Shawn Alexander
ISBN 978-1-59307-852-2 | $14.99

Conan: The Blood-Stained Crown and Other Stories
Kurt Busiek, Fabian Nicieza, Cary Nord, Eric Powell, Bruce Timm, and others
ISBN 978-1-59307-886-7 | $14.99

CONAN THE PHENOMENON

Paul M. Sammon
ISBN 978-1-59307-653-5 | $29.99

CONAN ONGOING SERIES

Volume 0: Born on the Battlefield
Kurt Busiek and Greg Ruth
TPB: ISBN 978-1-59307-981-9 | $17.99
HC: ISBN 978-1-59307-980-2 | $24.99

Volume 1: The Frost-Giant's Daughter and Other Stories
Kurt Busiek, Cary Nord, Tim Truman, and others
ISBN 978-1-59307-301-5 | $15.99

Volume 2: The God in the Bowl and Other Stories
Kurt Busiek and Cary Nord
ISBN 978-1-59307-403-6 | $15.99

Volume 3: The Tower of the Elephant and Other Stories
Kurt Busiek, Michael Wm. Kaluta, and Cary Nord
ISBN 978-1-59307-547-7 | $15.99

DarkHorse.com
AVAILABLE AT YOUR LOCAL COMICS SHOP OR BOOKSTORE | TO FIND A COMICS SHOP IN YOUR AREA, CALL 1-888-266-4226
For more information or to order direct: **On the web:** darkhorse.com **E-mail:** mailorder@darkhorse.com **Phone:** 1-800-862-0052 Mon.–Fri. 9 AM to 5 PM Pacific Time.

HE WORLDS OF ROBERT E. HOWARD

Dark Horse is proud to continue our tradition of bringing Robert E. Howard's incomparable characters to life!

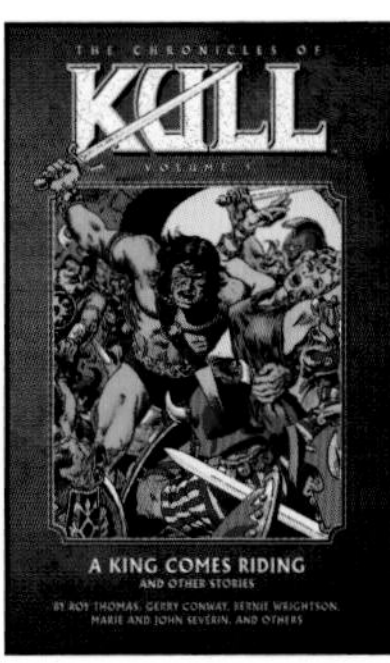

lume 4: The Hall of the Dead
d Other Stories
ırt Busiek, Mike Mignola,
n Truman, and Cary Nord
3N 978-1-59307-775-4 | $17.99

lume 5: Rogues in the House
d Other Stories
n Truman, Cary Nord, and Tomás Giorello
3N 978-1-59307-903-1 | $17.99

lume 6: The Hand of Nergal
n Truman and Tomás Giorello
B: ISBN 978-1-59582-178-2 | $17.99
:: ISBN 978-1-59582-179-9 | $24.99

lume 7: Cimmeria
m Truman, Tomás Giorello,
d Richard Corben
B: ISBN 978-1-59582-283-3 | $17.99
:: ISBN 978-1-59582-341-0 | $24.99

lume 8: Black Colossus
m Truman and Tomás Giorello
B: ISBN 978-1-59582-533-9 | $17.99
:: ISBN 978-1-59582-507-0 | $24.99

lume 9: Free Companions
m Truman, Tomás Giorello,
d Joe Kubert
B: ISBN 978-1-59582-592-6 | $17.99
:: ISBN 978-1-59582-623-7 | $24.99

lume 10: Iron Shadows in the Moon
m Truman, Tomás Giorello,
d Cary Nord
B: ISBN 978-1-59582-713-5 | $17.99
:: ISBN 978-1-59582-712-8 | $24.99

HE CHRONICLES OF KING CONAN

lume 1: The Witch of the Mists
d Other Stories
3N 978-1-59307-477-7 | $18.99

lume 2: Vengeance from the Desert
d Other Stories
3N 978-1-59582-670-1 | $18.99

THE SAVAGE SWORD OF CONAN

Roy Thomas, Barry Windsor-Smith, John Buscema, Alfredo Alcala, Pablo Marcos, and others

Volume 1: ISBN 978-1-59307-838-6 | $17.99
Volume 2: ISBN 978-1-59307-894-2 | $17.99
Volume 3: ISBN 978-1-59307-960-4 | $19.99
Volume 4: ISBN 978-1-59582-149-2 | $19.99
Volume 5: ISBN 978-1-59582-175-1 | $19.99
Volume 6: ISBN 978-1-59582-375-5 | $19.99
Volume 7: ISBN 978-1-59582-510-0 | $19.99
Volume 9: ISBN 978-1-59582-648-0 | $19.99
Volume 10: ISBN 978-1-59582-799-9 | $19.99

KULL™

THE CHRONICLES OF KULL

Roy Thomas, Wallace Wood, Gerry Conway, Len Wein, Bernie Wrightson, Marie Severin, Ed Hannigan, Don Glut, and others

Volume 1: A King Comes Riding and Other Stories
ISBN 978-1-59582-413-4 | $18.99

Volume 2: The Hell Beneath Atlantis and Other Stories
ISBN 978-1-59582-439-4 | $18.99

Volume 3: Screams in the Dark and Other Stories
ISBN 978-1-59582-585-8 | $18.99

Volume 4: The Blood of Kings and Other Stories
ISBN 978-1-59582-684-8 | $18.99

KULL MINISERIES

Arvid Nelson, Will Conrad, and José Villarrubia

Volume 1: The Shadow Kingdom
ISBN 978-1-59582-385-4 | $18.99

Volume 2: The Hate Witch
ISBN 978-1-59582-730-2 | $15.99

THE SAVAGE SWORD OF KULL

Roy Thomas, Bernie Wrightson, Howard Chaykin, Barry Windsor-Smith, and others

Volume 1: ISBN 978-1-59582-593-3 | $19.99
Volume 2: ISBN 978-1-59582-788-3 | $19.99

THE CHRONICLES OF SOLOMON KANE

Written by Roy Thomas and Ralph Macchio
Art by Howard Chaykin, Al Williamson, Mike Mignola, and others
ISBN 978-1-59582-410-3 | $18.99

THE SAGA OF SOLOMON KANE

Written by Robert E. Howard, Roy Thomas, Don Glut, and others
Art by Neal Adams, Al Williamson, Bill Wray, and others
ISBN 978-1-59582-317-5 | $19.99

SOLOMON KANE MINISERIES

Roy Thomas, Bernie Wrightson, Howard Chaykin, Barry Windsor-Smith, and others

Volume 1: The Castle of the Devil
ISBN 978-1-59582-282-6 | $15.99

Volume 2: Death's Black Riders
ISBN 978-1-59582-590-2 | $15.99

DarkHorse.com
AVAILABLE AT YOUR LOCAL COMICS SHOP OR BOOKSTORE | TO FIND A COMICS SHOP IN YOUR AREA, CALL 1-888-266-4226
For more information or to order direct: **On the web:** darkhorse.com **E-mail:** mailorder@darkhorse.com **Phone:** 1-800-862-0052
Mon.–Fri. 9 AM to 5 PM Pacific Time.